SpringerBriefs in Archaeology

Series editors:
Douglas Comer
Helaine Silverman
Willem Willems

Robert J. Shepherd • Larry Yu

Heritage Management, Tourism, and Governance in China

Managing the Past to Serve the Present

 Springer

Robert J. Shepherd
The George Washington University
Washington, DC, USA

Larry Yu
The George Washington University
Washington, DC, USA

ISSN 1861-6623   ISSN 2192-4910 (electronic)
ISBN 978-1-4614-5917-0 ISBN 978-1-4614-5918-7 (eBook)
DOI 10.1007/978-1-4614-5918-7
Springer New York Heidelberg Dordrecht London

Library of Congress Control Number: 2012951417

© Springer Science+Business Media, LLC 2013
This work is subject to copyright. All rights are reserved by the Publisher, whether the whole or part of the material is concerned, specifically the rights of translation, reprinting, reuse of illustrations, recitation, broadcasting, reproduction on microfilms or in any other physical way, and transmission or information storage and retrieval, electronic adaptation, computer software, or by similar or dissimilar methodology now known or hereafter developed. Exempted from this legal reservation are brief excerpts in connection with reviews or scholarly analysis or material supplied specifically for the purpose of being entered and executed on a computer system, for exclusive use by the purchaser of the work. Duplication of this publication or parts thereof is permitted only under the provisions of the Copyright Law of the Publisher's location, in its current version, and permission for use must always be obtained from Springer. Permissions for use may be obtained through RightsLink at the Copyright Clearance Center. Violations are liable to prosecution under the respective Copyright Law.
The use of general descriptive names, registered names, trademarks, service marks, etc. in this publication does not imply, even in the absence of a specific statement, that such names are exempt from the relevant protective laws and regulations and therefore free for general use.
While the advice and information in this book are believed to be true and accurate at the date of publication, neither the authors nor the editors nor the publisher can accept any legal responsibility for any errors or omissions that may be made. The publisher makes no warranty, express or implied, with respect to the material contained herein.

Printed on acid-free paper

Springer is part of Springer Science+Business Media (www.springer.com)

We dedicate this book to our life companions, Sarah Chen (Larry) and Fithri Ekawati (Robert).

Acknowledgments

We would like to thank Douglas C. Comer, Helaine Silverman, and Willem J. H. Willems, editors of the International Committee on Archaeological Management's book series on archeological heritage management, along with Teresa Krauss, series general editor with Springer Press, for providing us this opportunity. In addition, we are grateful for generous research funding provided by the Sigur Center for Asian Studies at the George Washington University that helped us complete this project. We would also like to thank our student research assistants at GWU, Wu Xiaoxiao and Hu Yihan, for their fine work. In addition, we are grateful for field research assistance provided in the summer of 2010 by Professor Gu Huimin of Beijing International Studies University as well as her student assistants, Mu Xiaoting, Chen Yuting, Lü Jiayu, Tong Yao, and Pan Zhiren. Finally, we are grateful to the anonymous reviewers who provided valuable comments that have helped us strengthen our narrative.

Contents

1 Introduction 1
Bibliography 4

2 Historical Background 5
Bibliography 10

3 The Politics of Heritage 13
Bibliography 30

4 Nature, Culture, and Civilization 33
Bibliography 44

5 Economics of Heritage Management 47
The Administrative Structure... 48
Management of Cultural Heritage 50
The Admissions Economy Phenomenon 57
Bibliography 64

6 The Social Impact of Heritage 67
The Paradox of Heritage Preservation 69
Creating Heritage 72
Development Versus Heritage.. 74
Becoming a Tourist Attraction.. 76
Bibliography 81

Conclusion 85
Bibliography 86

Index 87

List of Figures

Fig. 2.1   Sun Yat-sen, leader of the nationalist movement that
established the Republic of China in 1911
(National Museum of China, Beijing)   9

Fig. 3.1   Museum of Natural History, Beijing, built in 1951   14
Fig. 3.2   Imagining a multiethnic historic China: interpretive panel,
National Museum of China, Beijing   22
Fig. 3.3   Diorama of nationalist revolutionaries attacking Qing forces
in 1911 (National Museum of China, Beijing)   23
Fig. 3.4   "Fire on the Grasslands": war against Japan exhibit,
Inner Mongolia Museum, Hohhot, 2009..   24
Fig. 3.5   Tomb of Wang Zhaojun (first century BCE),
one of China's "Four Ancient Beauties," near Hohhot,
Inner Mongolia...   29
Fig. 3.6   The state protects history? Signs such as these are common
at Chinese heritage sites...   30

Fig. 4.1   "Establishing civility requires everyone's participation":
banner along a pedestrian walkway in suburban Beijing, 2011.......   38
Fig. 4.2   The refurbished Sumtseling (Songzanlin) Monastery (built 1659),
the largest Tibetan Buddhist monastery in Yunnan, located
in Zhongdian County (*Tibetan Gyalthung*). The complex
was shelled by People's Liberation Army Forces in 1959
and attacked by Red Guards during the Cultural Revolution   41
Fig. 4.3   The newly built Wenshu (Manjusri) Temple, Mount Wutai,
Shanxi, a world heritage site   42

Fig. 5.1   Yungang Grottoes (fifth century CE), Datong, Shanxi
province, a 5A national scenic site...   49
Fig. 5.2   The Great Wall near Mutianyu, Beijing municipality.
This section of the Wall was originally built during
the sixth century CE..   53

Fig. 5.3   Tayuan Temple (sixteenth century), Mount Wutai,
              Shanxi province   54
Fig. 5.4   Long Lake, Jiuzhaigou National Park, Sichuan province   56
Fig. 5.5   Street Scene, Lijiang, Yunnan province   58
Fig. 5.6   Nine-story pagoda (built in 1751), Qing Imperial
              Mountain Resort, Chengde, Hebei province.....................................   63

Fig. 6.1   Tour group waiting to enter the Forbidden City, Beijing, 2010........   69
Fig. 6.2   Dozens of local homes were demolished in Taihuai,
              Mount Wutai, after the area became a national park and a world
              heritage site in 2010..   71
Fig. 6.3   The "New Qianmen," looking north toward the front gate
              to the Forbidden City, Beijing, 2011...   72
Fig. 6.4   Xintiandi, Shanghai: once a working class neighborhood,
              now a trendy entertainment district...   73
Fig. 6.5   Becoming a tourist attraction: the recently built Tibetan Quarter
              in Jiantang, Zhongdian County (renamed "Shangri La" in 2001),
              Yunnan province   78

Chapter 1
Introduction

This monograph analyzes current cultural resource management, archeological heritage management, and exhibition practices and policies in the People's Republic of China, where state officials, preservationists, and other interested parties seek to balance the needs and demands of heritage preservation with rapid economic and social changes. On the one hand, state-supported development policies and projects often threaten and in some cases lead to the destruction of archeological and cultural sites. On the other hand, current national cultural policies also encourage the preservation, renovation, and in some situations reconstruction of precisely such sites as heritage and tourism destinations that can serve as development resources. Underlining this paradox is a key political quandary. Over the past two decades, the Chinese Communist Party (CCP) has abandoned the core tenants of Maoist revolutionary socialism (an emphasis on class struggle, collectivism, and public ownership of the means of production) in favor of neoliberal policies that emphasize personal responsibility, economic efficiency, and the efficacy of market forces in shaping society. As a result, the post-1949 state historical narrative utilized to explain China's past at museums, historic sites, and other cultural spaces has been reshaped, since a temporal narrative rooted in socialist ideology no longer explains the current social reality of China, which includes a growing class divide, a scaling back of state services, and a party-encouraged focus on mass consumption. The central government's challenge is to manage this transformation in a way that justifies continued CCP rule (Denton 2005). As part of this process, both the Communist Party and the national-level state have deemphasized global socialism in favor of cultural nationalism and highlighted the current government's efforts to protect and preserve China's long historical past in the two decades since popular protests erupted in the spring of 1989 (Hevia 2001; Lee 2008). It is for these reasons that "heritage" (*yichan*), although a relatively recent neologism first promoted by the CCP in 1982, has become a crucial part of the political process in contemporary China. And the personal experiencing of this shared tangible and intangible storehouse of knowledge is the basis of the rapidly expanding domestic tourism industry in the PRC (Sofield and Li 1998: 367).

R.J. Shepherd and L. Yu, *Heritage Management, Tourism, and Governance in China: Managing the Past to Serve the Present*, SpringerBriefs in Archaeology 2, DOI 10.1007/978-1-4614-5918-7_1, © Springer Science+Business Media, LLC 2013

Researchers in anthropology, sociology, museum studies, tourist studies, and related disciplines have, in recent years, analyzed the emergence of a "new Cultural Revolution" in the PRC during the late reform period. This includes work on world heritage sites (Hevia 2001; Nyiri 2006), national tourism policies (Sofield and Li 1998, 2009; Shepherd 2008), ethnic tourism (Oakes 1997; Hillmen 2003; Shepherd 2006), and museum display (Denton 2005). The post-1990 reform period has seen a steady rise in personal incomes, the emergence of a middle class with disposable incomes, unprecedented freedom of movement for citizens, and a renewed interest among people in the pre-PRC past made possible by a Communist Party retreat from the private sphere. The net result has been an explosion in the heritage and tourism industries. In this book, we discuss these rapid changes and the tensions and conflicts between proponents of tourism, heritage preservation, economic development, a new class of wealthy elites with the means to buy and collect historical artifacts, and a fragmented regulatory system.

Despite its wide popularity throughout the world, "heritage" is an extremely broad and loosely defined term. It is used to describe not just material culture such as archeological sites, monuments, memorials, buildings, sculpture, paintings, and other artifacts but also literature, poetry, philosophy, language, sports, and the performative arts (Nuryanti 1996: 252). It is also an ideological concept, one which Tim Winter and Patrick Daly suggest is a moral imperative linked to an inherent suspicion of change (2011: 9). Once labeled as heritage, a place, object, or practice is implicitly tied to a presumed division between its realness and a destructive market process (Svensson 2006). Heritage is thus an encounter of time (past and present), materiality (the ontologically authentic and the market-driven copy), and use value. Whatever its form, heritage is an interpretive process, with meanings generated by those in a position to make a heritage claim and aimed at an intended audience. Without such an audience, a heritage claim is of little use. Hence, like museums, heritage succeeds to the extent that it is able to attract an audience.

Our focus in this book is on Chinese tangible heritage sites, which China's State Administration of Cultural Heritage (SACH) estimates to number more than 400,000. An examination of material artifacts is important because this provides insight into the society which produced these. At the same time, material objects shape cultural practices, providing insight into how people of a specific time and place viewed life (Kieschnick 2003: 15). We thus include in our use of "heritage" archeological artifacts and sites; religious structures; state buildings such as monuments and memorials; historically important built space such as urban neighborhoods, town and city walls, gates, bell towers, and parks; and aesthetic objects such as paintings, scrolls, and sculptures.

We do not discuss the intangible cultural practices of China, mainly because of space limitations and the ambiguity of what constitutes an intangible heritage practice. The United Nation's 2003 *Convention on Intangible Heritage* defines intangible heritage as "practices, representations, expressions, knowledge, skills – as well as the instruments, objects, artifacts and cultural spaces associated therewith – that communities, groups and, in some cases, individuals recognize as part of their cultural heritage" (UNESCO 2003). The broadness of this statement suggests that most any cultural practice can be classified as "intangible heritage." Thus, for example, in a 2012 temporary exhibit entitled "Beijing's Intangible Cultural Heritage" at China's National Museum of History, kite-making, calligraphy, and flute-making techniques were displayed beside an oversized bottle of Red Star brand *Er Guo Tou*, a sorghum-based alcohol produced in the city, and shoulder massaging, touted as unique to Beijing.

The simultaneous display of kites, hard liquor, and calligraphy illustrates the cultural arbitrariness of what counts as intangible heritage. At the time the *Convention for the Safekeeping of Intangible Cultural Heritage* took effect in 2006, the Chinese government already had nominated 518 examples of intangible practices in ten different categories, ranging from folk music, drama, and dance to handicraft skills, traditional medicines, and acrobatics (China Heritage Quarterly 2006). Collecting and categorizing cultural practices in China has its roots in the New Cultural Movement of the 1920s and state-directed ethnohistory projects in the 1950s. To date, the PRC has conducted three national cultural practices surveys. The first occurred in the 1950s at the same time that the new government undertook a national ethnic survey, the second in 1982 when national laws on heritage were decreed, and the most recent in 2007 (Shen and Chen 2010: 74). These surveys have classified thousands of folk (*minsu*) practices, all of which theoretically fall under the domain of intangible heritage. At the international level, the lack of adequate criteria for judging what counts as "intangible" heritage led to the suspension of the convention governing these shortly after this took effect. This confusion has had little impact in China, where various practices continue to be classified under a 2004 "Preservation Program of the National and Folk Culture of China." Moreover, as will be discussed later, there is no contradiction from a Chinese perspective in simultaneously seeking world heritage status for a particular cultural folk practice and using this practice as a tourist resource. We will therefore focus on tangible heritage sites and practices, characterized by Mary Hancock (2008) as public memory sites, either real or desired, as evoked by state actors or cultural brokers.

Finally, we wish to make note of the significant and very real changes in the culture industries that have taken place in China in the last two decades. Field researchers have far greater autonomy, Maoist ideology no longer trumps scientific inquiry, and hundreds of millions of Chinese citizens now have the ability to personally experience cultural and historical sites around the country. These transformational changes, often ignored by international critics, have fundamentally changed the cultural landscape in the PRC. They also raise additional questions about accessibility and carrying capacity for sites that few if any societies have ever had to address. For example, in a country of approximately 1.3 billion people, should all have access to fragile cultural and natural sites? What limits, if any, should be placed on visitors? What role should market forces play in answering these questions? These issues go to the heart of the heritage debate in today's China.

Bibliography

China Heritage Quarterly. 2006. China's intangible cultural heritage (Editorial). *China Heritage Quarterly* 7, September 2006. Canberra: China Heritage Project, Australian National University.

Denton, Kirk. 2005. Museums, memorial sites and exhibitionary culture in the People's Republic of China. *China Quarterly* 183(September): 565–586.

Hancock, Mary. 2008. *The politics of heritage from Madras to Chennai*. Bloomington: University of Indiana.

Hevia, James. 2001. World heritage, national culture, and the restoration of Chengde. *Positions* 9(1): 219–243.

Hillmen, Ben. 2003. Paradise under construction: Minorities, myths, and modernity in northwest Yunnan. *Asian Ethnicity* 4(2): 175–188.

Kieschnick, John. 2003. *The Impact of Buddhism on Chinese Material Culture*. Princeton, NJ: Princeton University Press.

Lee Haiyan. 2008. The ruins of *Yuangmingyuan* or, how to enjoy a national wound. *Modern China* 20(10): 1–36.

Li Fung Mei, and Trevor Sofield. 2009. Huangshan (Yellow Mountain), China: The meaning of harmonious relationships. In *Tourism in China: Destinations, cultures, and communities*, ed. Chris Ryan and Gu Huimin, 157–167. London: Routledge.

Nuryanti, Wiendu. 1996. Heritage and postmodern tourism. *Annals of Tourism Research* 23(2): 249–260.

Nyiri, Pal. 2006. *Scenic spots: Chinese tourism, the state, and cultural authority*. Seattle: University of Washington.

Oakes, Timothy. 1997. Ethnic Tourism in Rural Guizhou: Sense of Place and the Commerce of Authenticity. In *Tourism, ethnicity, and the state in Asian and Pacific societies*, ed. Michel Picard and Robert Wood, 35–70. Honolulu: University of Hawai'i Press.

Shen, Chen, and Hong Chen. 2008. Cultural heritage, UNESCO, and the Chinese State: Whose heritage and for whom? *Heritage Management* 2(1): 55–79.

Shen, Chen, and Hong Chen. 2010. Cultural heritage management in China: Current practices and problems. In *Cultural heritage management: A global perspective*, ed. Phyllis Messenger and George Smith, 70–81. Gainesville: University of Florida.

Shepherd, Robert. 2006. UNESCO and the politics of cultural heritage in Tibet. *Journal of Contemporary Asia* 36(2): 243–257.

Shepherd, Robert. 2008 "Cultural Heritage, UNESCO, and the Chinese State: Whose Heritage and for Whom?" *Heritage Management* 2:1, 55–79.

Sofield, Trevor, and Fung Mei Li. 1998. Tourism development and cultural policies in China. *Annals of Tourism Research* 25(2): 362–392.

Svensson, Marina. 2006. In the ancestor's shadow: Cultural heritage contestations in Chinese villages. Working paper #16. Stockholm: Centre for East and Southeast Asian Studies, Lund University.

UNESCO. 2003. Convention for the safeguarding of intangible cultural heritage. Electronic document. http://www.unesco.org/culture/ich/index.php?pg=00006. Accessed 28 June 2012.

Winter, Tim, and Patrick Daly. 2011. Heritage in Asia: Converging forces, conflicting values. In *Routledge handbook of heritage in Asia*, ed. Patrick Daly and Tim Winter, 1–35. London: Routledge Press.

Chapter 2
Historical Background

Tangible objects have served both cosmological and political purposes in China since the Zhou dynastic era (approximately 1,000–250 BCE). In order to assert their own legitimacy, rulers typically would display the bronze and jade ritual objects as well as court seals, scrolls, and tax records of either their ancestors or those whom they had defeated. For the same reason, rulers would attempt to monopolize production of these objects (Elliot and Shambaugh 2005: 5–6). What we now know as "heritage objects" were thus originally collected, preserved, and displayed in China for contemporary political purposes, not because they reflected the past per se or for their aesthetic value. Instead, these imperial objects were believed to enable a communicative link with heaven (see Chang 1983). For example, following their conquest of the Song capital of Kaifeng in 1127 AD, the Jurchen, a seminomadic group from Manchuria, looted the imperial warehouses of art, furniture, scrolls, paintings, musical instruments, and even clothing, all of which they transported to their own capital, present-day Beijing, where they established the Jin Dynasty. The Jurchen capital was in turn conquered by the Mongolian leader Genghis Khan in 1234 AD, who named the city Dadu and built a palace on the site of what is now Beihai Park (Elliot and Shambaugh 2005: 24–28). Similarly, when Zhu Yuanzhang, founder of the Ming Dynasty (1368–1644), overthrew the Mongolian Yuan Dynasty (1271–1368), his forces seized control of an imperial collection that contained artifacts dating from the ninth-century Tang. After this, he ordered the destruction of the Yuan palaces in Beijing and transported these artifacts to his new capital at Nanjing, only to have the third Ming Emperor, Zhu Di, shift the capital back to Beijing in 1421, following the construction of the Forbidden City between 1406 and 1420.

This chapter describes the development of archeology, heritage, and museums in China. By way of introduction, we review the purpose and methods of traditional historiography, the cultivation of an interest among elites in the past during the Song, Ming, and Qing eras, the role of cultural heritage in the late Qing and Republican periods, and the place of history and heritage in the civil war between Communists and Nationalists. We also introduce the key concept of jingdian ("scenic spot") and discuss their role in the development of a national class of literati and scholars dating back to at least the Ming Dynasty (1368–1644).

R.J. Shepherd and L. Yu, *Heritage Management, Tourism, and Governance in China: Managing the Past to Serve the Present*, SpringerBriefs in Archaeology 2, DOI 10.1007/978-1-4614-5918-7_2, © Springer Science+Business Media, LLC 2013

As these examples show, as each succeeding group overthrew existing rulers, they would seek to capture the material objects of authority, at times destroy the built space of those whom they had defeated, and relocate the center of power. This is a pattern that would continue until the 1911 Revolution, when the new Nationalist government led by the revolutionary hero Dr. Sun Yat-sen moved the capital from Beijing to Nanjing. This also illustrates how what we refer to as "China" has not been a fixed territorial space. Instead, the territory of this entity has shifted with each conquest, expanding and contracting, while the center of power has followed each conqueror. Chinese archeologists have identified as many as 13 different dynastic capitals, ranging from Beijing, Nanjing, and Xian to Datong, Kaifeng, and Luoyang.

This also demonstrates the political importance of material culture in China for thousands of years. Objects from the past were important because they were believed to legitimize new rulers. However, although field archeology is relatively new in China, the study of past dynasties through an analysis of their material artifacts is not, dating back to the Song Dynasty (960–1279 AD). What K.C. Chang termed an antiquarian interest in the past can be traced to two key works, the *Kaogutu* (1092) by Lu Dalin (1046–1092) and the *Bogutu* (1107) by Wang Fu (1079–1126). These were catalogues that provided drawings and descriptions of bronze and jade objects from previous eras, including private as well as imperial collections (Chang 1981: 156–158).[1]

Similarly, travel as an exercise in experiential learning and enjoyment dates back to at least Confucius (551–479 BCE), who spent much of his adult life traveling between states in search of a just ruler to serve. Tellingly, the roots of the Chinese term for travel (*luyou*) are not in physical exertion and work (*travail*) as in Romance languages but in fun, companionship, and entertainment (Han 2006: 83). Beginning in the late Tang Dynasty (618–907) and continuing during the Song Dynasty, well-to-do literati traveled to famous sites. These sites, variously known as *jingshen* (scenic spots), *fengjing qu* ("wind and scenes"), and *mingshen qu* (famous sites), date as far back as the Qin Dynasty (Nyiri 2006: 7). By the sixteenth century, a canon of such sites had emerged. These were visited to confirm interpretations handed down by Tang and Song era predecessors, primarily through written and visual markers (Strassberg 1994). For example, sites would typically be characterized as resembling animals, people, or other objects and marked by poetry or at times by literal inscriptions carved on rocks. There was little if any focus on personal interpretation; sites were judged on the extent to which they fulfilled and confirmed a shared interpretation: "Views – even in their names – encompassed not only a particular aspect of a scenic spot, but also the appropriate circumstances of viewing, which could include season, time of the day, weather and the spectator's mood" (Nyiri 2006: 9).

Completely absent from this Chinese approach to travel was any romanticized notion of solitary travel as intrinsically superior. Indeed, the idea of traveling alone in circumstances designed to force the traveler to confront radical differences and alienation from the familiar as a means of gaining new insights has never been part

---

[1] Lu Dalin has been hailed by state authorities as China's first anthropologist. In 2010, his tomb, along with those of several relatives, was excavated in Lantian County, near Xian in Shaanxi province (Yang 2010).

of mainstream Chinese norms. This was true for monasteries as well. Pilgrimage destinations such as Mount Wutai (*Wutai Shan*) in Shanxi, Mount Emei (*Emeishan*) in Sichuan, and Yellow Mountain (*Huangshan*) in Anhui provinces were economic, social, and tourist centers and thus part of everyday life (Kieschnick 2003: 186–187). Travel in China today remains overwhelmingly a social activity, undertaken with friends and family, as we discuss in Chap. 6. It also remains focused on *jingshan*. However, what counts as a scenic spot continues to expand: no longer limited to classical sites, the list of national "must-see" destinations now includes classical, early modern, Republican era, civil war, Maoist, and even modern sites such as theme parks and shopping malls.

The emergent interest, particularly during the Song and Ming eras, in studying the past through material cultural and travel remained subservient, however, to a much broader and deeper historiography. The underlying purpose of studying the past throughout Chinese history has been to document proper and improper behavior, identify the just and the unjust, and thereby influence action in the present. The practice of history was not a faithful recounting of facts; it was a moral project. And until the twentieth century, the primary form this took was biographical (Chang 1981: 157). For example, during the Tang era, an official history office was established to document and interpret previous reigns. The intent was not necessarily to establish what really happened or what was "true" but for "bureaucrats to justify the present dynasty's power and authority" (Fowler 1987: 238).

How does this relate to a sense of national identity? A common view is that identification as "Chinese" is a very new phenomenon and only began to emerge in the years immediately before and following the 1911 Revolution. However, others argue that a key result of the Jin and Mongol conquests between the twelve and fourteenth centuries was an increased consciousness among elites of a civilized self standing in contrast to a suspect not-civilized other. Following the Manchurian invasion and defeat of the Ming rulers in 1644 and the establishment of the Qing Dynasty (1644–1911), this emergent sense of "Chineseness" was directed against Manchu authorities (Duara 1993: 5). Some scholars go further, arguing that the material record demonstrates a relatively wide geographical space of similitude. K.C. Chang cites the Shang Dynasty (1,766–1,027 BCE) as an example. If the extent of this state is defined by evidence of writing, then the Shang territories were relatively small. If, however, the Shang sphere is defined by archeological discoveries of bronze and pottery, then this state stretched from Liaoning in the north as far south as Hunan (Chang 1977: 640).

Nevertheless, in hindsight, it is clear that one of the key problems faced by Sun Yat-sen and his colleagues in their ethno-nationalist campaign against authorities in the final years of the Qing Dynasty was a noticeable absent of National identity among people. Indeed, most subjects of the Qing Empire did not identify as either "Chinese" or as "Han" but by kin, place, or language ties. This lack of a cohesive ethno-nationalist identity reflected foundational Confucian attributes that classified people not by race, ethnicity, or place of birth but by their degree of cultural achievement. From a Confucian perspective, people were not Chinese or other; they were civilized or other. Anyone could become Chinese by acquiring the language skills needed to access Confucian texts that in turn instruct in how to be a person capable of cultivating *ren*, the foundational human condition of virtue, benevolence, and proper social behavior. To cultivate *ren* is to cultivate one's human essence and thus to be human(e). Until the late nineteenth century, this Sino-centric world view simply assumed that outsiders, if given an opportunity, would want to be transformed into civilized (e.g., fully human, hence "Chinese") people, since to not be Chinese was by definition, to be inferior (Zhang 1997: 76). Being Chinese was thus a cultural category, not biological or even historical, and was achieved not by dint of birth but through education and self-reflection.

Confronted with this dilemma, a society of people who lacked a national consciousness, Sun Yat-sen's Tong Meng Hui (Chinese United League), the forerunner of the Nationalist Party (KMT), promoted the concept of Han nationality or ethnicity (*minzu*). The first of Sun Yat-sen's "Three Principles of the People" (*Sanmin Zhuyi*) *minzu* was a transliteration of the Japanese neologism *minzokushugi*, which became prevalent in Japan after the Meiji Restoration and connoted racial uniqueness (Tuttle 2005; Zhang 1997). Sun Yat-sen argued that the subjects of the Qing had to be convinced they were not just historically linked to a ethno-national past as "people of the Han" (*Han ren*) but also biologically linked to each other as a "Han race" (*Han minzu*). According to Sun, only after recognizing this would Qing subjects recognize the Qing state as a foreign occupation (Gladney 2004: 13–14). In other words, for a Nationalist revolution to succeed, the foundational Confucian emphasis on the five relationships (*wulun*) had to be broken. Rather than defining themselves according to ties with their spouses, children, parents, friends, and ruler, Qing subjects had to be convinced to identify with other subjects with whom they presumably shared a *zu*, a hazy concept that translates as clan, community, or ethnic group but for Sun's purposes defined one's race (Dikötter 1992: 123). Only when this was achieved would the subjects of the empire see themselves as citizens of a republic (Harrison 2000: 175) (Fig. 2.1).[2]

Yet in the aftermath of the establishment of the Republic of China (1911-), Dr. Sun called on Han Chinese to transcend their (new) ethno-nationalist conscious and become the leaders of a multiethnic society of Chinese (*zhongguo ren*). This dual emphasis on the Han people as the vanguard of the revolution and a collective advance of all Chinese toward modernization has continued under the Chinese Communist Party, as we discuss in Chap. 4.

While the collecting and archiving of material artifacts have been a part of the historical record in China for more than two millennia, both the scientific search for and public display of objects are a relatively recent practice. The Geological Survey of China was established in 1916. This organization was dominated by Europeans

---

[2] Prasenjit Duara (1992) argues that the category of racial difference in fact appeared in China during the reign of the Qing Emperor Qianlong (1735–1796), who led an active campaign to codify Manchurian superiority by dint of birth. Duara also argues that the great Taiping Rebellion (1850–1864) was a Nationalist rebellion against Manchu control and led to a Manchu ethnic revival. Other scholars argue that the Taiping Rebellion was a religiously inspired charismatic movement, given that its leader, Hong Xiuquan, claimed to be the brother of Jesus Christ.

Fig. 2.1 Sun Yat-sen, leader of the nationalist movement that established the Republic of China in 1911 (National Museum of China, Beijing)

such as Johan Gunnar Andersson, who led the first archeological excavation of Paleolithic Yangshao sites in Henan province in 1921. However, these early field researchers were trained not in archeology but in geology and paleoanthropology. They consequently emphasized index fossils and comparative analysis across a wide geographical range rather than individual sites (Chang 1981: 164). The founder of scientific archeology in China is generally regarded as Li Chi (1895–1979). Li studied both ethnology and physical anthropology at Harvard before returning to China in 1921. He was the first Chinese scientist to work on a field excavation, joining the Yangshao dig in 1923. He later helped establish the first Archeology Department in China, at Beijing University in 1925, served as the first director of the Central History Museum in 1945, and served as the founding director of the Department of Archeology at National Taiwan University in 1949 (Chang 1981: 165).

The emergence of archeology as a field of study reflected a growing interest among Chinese scholars in empirically based sciences. In 1930, the KMT (Nationalist) government passed a *Law on the Preservation of Ancient Objects*, the country's first regulations of cultural artifacts (Murphy 2004; Zhuang 1989). This was followed in 1931 by the "Statute for the Preservation of Scenic Spots, Points of Historical Importance, and Articles of Historical, Cultural, and Artistic Value" (Gruber 2007: 272).

The country's first museum had been established in Shanghai by French priest Pierre Heude in 1868, followed in 1872 by the founding of the British Royal Asiatic Society, also in Shanghai. The first government museum was opened in 1912 by the

Ministry of Education in Beijing on the grounds of the former Imperial University, and in 1914, the Ministry of the Interior opened the Beijing Ancient Relics Exhibition Hall to display the more than 70,000-piece art collection of the Qing Dynasty royal family. By 1921, the fledgling Republic of China had 13 museums located in Beijing, Hubei, Shandong, Shanxi, Hebei, Jiangsu, Guangdong, and Yunnan (Pao 1966: 22–23). And, following the expulsion of the disposed Emperor Puyi in 1924, the Forbidden City was opened to the public as a museum on October 10, 1925 (Watson 1995: 8). Despite political instability, military conflict among various warlords, a weak central government, and economic problems, the museum industry flourished in Republican China. Indeed, by 1936, shortly before the outbreak of the second Sino-Japanese War (1937–1945), the Republic of China had 77 museums, 56 art galleries, and almost 100 conservatories (Pao 1966: 31). This period also saw the emergence of a nascent tourism industry; in 1922, the *Encyclopedia of Chinese Scenic Spots and Ancient Relics* (*Zhonghua Guangguo Mingsheng Guji Daguan*) was published (Nyiri 2006: 14).

The first formal attempt to categorize the country's material heritage occurred in 1948, shortly before the collapse of the Nationalist government, when professors at Qinghua University issued a list of 450 sites under the title of *A Brief List of Important Architectural Heritages in China*. However, a government project to build a national museum in Nanjing failed, primarily because of the war. Construction began in 1933. Between 1932 and 1936, approximately 20,000 crates of material were shipped from Beijing's Forbidden City to Nanjing for the museum. But before the museum could open, the staff and curators packed the most important objects, divided these into three separate shipments, and followed government ministries to Chongqing in Sichuan province in 1938. They briefly returned to Nanjing in 1946 after the Japanese surrender before following the Guomindang (KMT) into exile on Taiwan in 1948, where this collection became the basis of the National Palace Museum in Taipei, which opened in 1965.

The Palace Museum in turn became a key component of the post-civil war struggle for international status between Chiang Kaishek's Nationalist government on Taiwan and the new People's Republic of China led by Mao Zedong. The KMT government in Taiwan claimed to be the guardians of China's historical record against a radical regime bent on the wholesale destruction of the past, while the CCP government in Beijing depicted the removal of the Nanjing collection to Taiwan as an act of theft (Watson 1995: 11). Heritage, then, even before it was labeled as such, was an important factor in modern Chinese politics much like it had been for centuries before this at times of regime change.

Bibliography

Chang, Kwang Chih. 1977. "Chinese Archeology since 1949." *Journal of Asian Studies* 36(4): 623–646.
Chang, Kwang Chih. 1981. Archeology and Chinese historiography. *World Archeology* 13(2): 156–169.

Chang, Kwang Chih. 1983. *Art, myth and ritual: The path to political authority in ancient China.* Cambridge, MA: Harvard University Press.

Dikötter, Frank. 1992. *The discourse of race in modern China.* Palo Alto: Stanford University Press.

Duara, Prasenjit. 1993. Deconstructing the Chinese Nation. *Australian Journal of Chinese Affairs* 30: 1–26.

Elliot, Jeannette, with David Shambaugh. 2005. *The odyssey of China's imperial art treasures.* Seattle: University of Washington.

Fowler, Don. 1987. Uses of the past: Archeology in the service of the state. *American Antiquity* 52(2): 229–248.

Gladney, Dru. 2004. *Dislocating China: Reflections on Muslims, minorities and other subaltern subjects.* Chicago: University of Chicago.

Gruber, Stefan. 2007. Protecting China's cultural heritage sites in times of rapid change. *Asian Pacific Journal of Environment and Law* 253(10): 253–301.

Han, Feng. 2006. The Chinese view of nature: Tourism in China's scenic and historic interest areas. Dissertation. Queensland: Queensland University of Technology

Harrison, Henrietta. 2000. *The making of the republican citizen: Political ceremonies and symbolism in China 1911–1929.* New York: Oxford University Press.

Kieschnick, John. 2003. *The Impact of Buddhism on Chinese Material Culture.* Princeton, NJ: Princeton University Press.

Murphy, Rachel. 2004. "Turning Peasants into Modern Chinese Citizens: "Population Quality" Discourse, Demographic Transition, and Primary Education." China Quarterly 177: 1–20.

Nyiri, Pal. 2006. *Scenic spots: Chinese tourism, the state, and cultural authority.* Seattle: University of Washington.

Pao, Ignatius T.P. 1966. *A history of Chinese museums.* Collected papers on History and Art in China. Taipei: National Historical Museum.

Strassberg, Richard. 1994. *Inscribed landscapes: Travel writing from imperial China.* Berkeley: University of California Press.

Tuttle, Gray. 2005. *Tibetan Buddhists in the making of modern China.* New York: Columbia University Press.

Watson, Rubie. 1995. Palaces, museums, squares: Chinese national spaces. *Museum Anthropology* 19(2): 7–19.

Yang Fang. 2010. China unearths tomb of country's first known anthropologist. *Xinhua News Service*, January 28. http://news.xinhuanet.com/english2010/china/2010-01/28/c_13154544. htm. Accessed 26 Aug 2012.

Zhang Haiyang. 1997. Wrestling with the connotations of Chinese 'Minzu'. *Economic and Political Weekly*, July 26, pp. 74–84.

Zhuang Min, 1989. "The Administration of China's Archeological Heritage" in Henry Cleere (ed.) Archeological Heritage Management in the Modern World. Oxford: Unwin Hyman, 102–109.

Chapter 3
The Politics of Heritage

Heritage is often differentiated from history by its selectivity (Logan 2007: 34). While history seeks to explain the past, heritage is a filtered depiction of these events. However, as seen in Chap. 2, historiography in China was traditionally a moral project, centered on describing the lives of both the upright and the immoral in order to instruct people in how to live. This historical approach continued after the victory of the Chinese Communist Party against the Nationalists. Since the establishment of the People's Republic on October 1, 1949, the presentation, depiction, and interpretation of China's past have been a political and pedagogical project. Immediately following the defeat of the Nationalist government, all museums were nationalized and reorganized to reflect a strict linear view of Chinese history based on a historical materialist interpretation. Drawing on the work of Henry Lewis Morgan (1818–1881) and Fredrick Engels (1820–1895), this social evolutionary model took as self-evident a universally applicable linear view of history, in which all societies advanced through similar material stages of development. Practicing archeologists were expected to interpret their findings through this politically inspired prism. Moreover, because the Communist Party emphasized a particular ideological interpretation of the past, open inquiry or a nonpolitical analysis of

---

Heritage plays an important role in the Chinese Communist Party's promotion of cultural nationalism to fill a void left by the Party's abandonment of world revolutionary socialism and Maoist nationalism. We begin with a broad discussion of the links between political goals, nationalism, and archeology before turning to a specific focus on China. After an introduction to heritage policies in China following liberation in 1949, we turn to the impact of the Cultural Revolution on culture, both tangible and intangible, that marked the Cultural Revolution (1966–1976) and the reasons why the CCP has since embraced the promotion of cultural preservation. Of importance also is the use of heritage as a moral/educational tool. The Cultural Revolution not only resulted in immense damage to tangible culture and sites, this also significantly impacted society's collective memory of the past. The net result is that heritage sites, museums, and artifacts also serve a pedagogical purpose, to simultaneously educate visitors about the past and shape them as modern subjects in the present.

R.J. Shepherd and L. Yu, *Heritage Management, Tourism, and Governance in China:*
Managing the Past to Serve the Present, SpringerBriefs in Archaeology 2,
DOI 10.1007/978-1-4614-5918-7_3, © Springer Science+Business Media, LLC 2013

Fig. 3.1 Museum of Natural History, Beijing, built in 1951

findings was impossible (Keightley 1977: 124). As a discipline, archeology was defined as a subfield of history, which in turn was classified as a social science that provided objective facts.

The past was divided into five periods defined by the organization of society and the means of production. This historical materialist approach dated the beginning of history in China to approximately 5,000 BCE and the establishment of the Yangshao (5,000–3,000 BCE), a (arguably) matriarchal Neolithic culture in Hunan province that had been discovered in 1921 by the Swedish archeologist Johan Andersson (1874–1960). This was followed by the Lungshan (3,000–1,900 BCE), located along the Yellow River valley in Northwest China; the Shang (approximately 1,766–1,122 BCE) and Zhou (1,046–256 BCE), classified as the first centralized feudal states; the Imperial era (220 BCE–1,911 AD); and finally the era of "Popular Resistance" (1911–1949) to both the Nationalist government and Japanese invaders (Keightley 1977: 126) (Fig. 3.1).

Museums and historical sites were relevant only as teaching mediums for instructing citizens about the past as interpreted by the Party. They were thus not designed to support open inquiry or the pursuit of truth, but political objectives. In this sense, the Communist Party continued the historiographical tradition of the past, which emphasized not truth but morality, but with one caveat, all of history before 1949 was characterized as evil, and whatever cultural achievements had been achieved had occurred in spite of exploitative rulers, not because of them (Fowler 1987: 238). However, an inherent tension underlined this historical approach. The Maoist revolutionary project sought to transcend both a feudal past that had weakened society and led to foreign attacks and national humiliation from 1842 to 1949 *and* the so-called historical laws of Marxism, which dictate that a feudal society necessarily must advance through fixed stages of development (including capitalism) before it could achieve socialism. Thus, while socialist ideology prevented rapid modernization, China's deep culture of particularism, rooted in kin and clan ties, undermined socialism (Sofield and Li 1998). Mao's response to this dilemma was his dictum to "use the past to serve the present." For example, in a letter, he wrote in 1964 to students at the Central Conservatory of Music in Beijing, Mao urged them to "make the past serve the present, and make foreign things serve China" (*guwei jinyong*). In this phrase, Mao combined two key elements of how the past had historically been interpreted in pre-1949 China. "To make the past serve the present" was a continuation of the traditional historical approach to past events, in which history was seen primarily as a moral, not a truth project, focused on highlighting the just and the unjust, the good and the bad, and those on the right side of history and those who were not. "To make foreign things serve China" (in the students' case, European-derived classical music) was a restatement of the *ti-yong* arguments that predated the 1911 Revolution: to utilize (*yong*) foreign practices, knowledge, and objects while maintaining the essence (*ti*) of "Chineseness."

When applied to the material artifacts of Chinese history, this Maoist dictum led to the selective erasure of some cultural sites and their replacement with new symbols of state power (Wu 2005). For example, historic areas to the south of the Forbidden City were demolished in 1958–1959 during the construction of the Great Hall of the People and expansion of Tiananmen Square, while Beijing's Ming-era walls were destroyed during construction of the city's first subway line between 1965 and 1969. However, state authorities also preserved some historic sites as examples of prerevolutionary feudalism. Thus, in Lhasa, capital of Tibet, the Dalai Lama's former summer palace (Norbulingka) was opened to the public as a museum dedicated to his supposedly extravagant lifestyle shortly after he went into exile in 1959, while the house on Gulangyu Island near Xiamen, Fujian province where Nationalist leader Chiang Kaishek stayed the night before he fled China in 1949, was maintained as a symbol of the defeat of the old regime.

Shortly after liberation, the State Council issued a decree in May 1950 that ordered the protection of historical sites, artifacts, books, and endangered animals (Zhuang 1989: 102). A decade later, in November 1961, the State Council issued the *Provisional Regulations on the Protection and Administration of Cultural Relics*, the country's first formal decree aimed at cultural preservation. This decree also established a national Cultural Relics Bureau (*wenwu zhengji zu*) within the Ministry of Culture to categorize and collect important cultural objects. In 1962, this Bureau published China's first list of national cultural sites. Numbering 180, these were classified as either "patriotic education bases" [*aiguo zhuyi jiaoyu jidi*] or "national protected work unit sites" [*guojia wenwu baohu danwei*] (Svensson 2006: 7). The former were mainly historical sites connected to the Communist

Party, while the latter included sites such as tombs, grottoes, buildings, and stone carvings that predated the collapse of Qing authority (Liu 1983: 97).[1]

This early focus on ethnicity and cultural protection was, however, vastly different than contemporary neoliberal projects aimed at highlighting multiculturalism and cultural diversity. The Chinese Communist Party took as self-evident the belief that ethnic and therefore cultural differences would disappear as a society progressed toward socialism and communism. Therefore, between 1949 and 1957, the Party supported the classification of ethnic groups, the establishment of minority research institutes, and the creation of scripts for various minority languages as a means toward furthering socialism and documenting cultural differences that Marxist theory assumed would soon disappear (Zhang Haiyang 1997: 76).

This attempt to create a national cultural heritage system was disrupted first by Mao's "Great Leap Forward" (1958–1961) and then by the Cultural Revolution (1966–1976). The former campaign was aimed at transcending Marxist historical stages and moving China from an agrarian-based feudal society to an industrialized socialist society in a generation. Putting into practice Mao's belief that Marxist stages of history could be skipped and communism achieved through sheer will power, millions of people were put to work to raise industrial output and food production. This utopian campaign ended in abysmal failure with as many as 30 million deaths primarily caused by mass famine (Dikötter 2010).

This also led to a Party shift away from Mao's radicalism in favor of a more pragmatic approach to governance. As a way of regaining his standing within the Party hierarchy, Mao unleashed the Cultural Revolution and turned his followers against both the Party and state.

The Cultural Revolution is generally portrayed as an Orwellian campaign of violence and destruction spurred by Mao Zedong's encouragement of youthful Red Guards to attack the "four olds" (customs, culture, habits, and ideas). Between the beginning of the Cultural Revolution in 1966 and Mao's death a decade later, thousands of historic sites including temples, churches, mosques, and other buildings were looted, destroyed, or turned into warehouses and other public buildings; private homes were ransacked; and "tradition" was effectively banned.

Without downplaying the enormous harm done to people and property, two points need to be considered in analyzing the impact the Cultural Revolution had on cultural heritage. First, this was not the first instance of ruling authorities directing the destruction of material culture, in either "new" or "old" China. A similar process of CCP-inspired attacks on the material record of the past had occurred during the land reform campaign conducted immediately after the establishment of the PRC in 1949. During this earlier campaign, a great many antiques, books, and other objects were looted and destroyed (Tong 1995: 193). Before this, the most often cited example of a state-directed attack on material culture occurred in 845 AD, when the

---

[1] This list included 33 Communist Party revolutionary sites, 14 grottoes, 11 stone carvings, 19 tombs of famous people, 77 historical buildings, and 26 archeological sites (Liu 1987: 97).

Wuzong Emperor directed the destruction of an estimated 4,600 Buddhist temples and 40,000 shrines. During this campaign, imperial authorities ordered the seizure and melting down of all Buddhist statues and directed imperial funding to Daoist temples and monasteries. This was thus not an attack on icons but on what the Emperor believed was a foreign religion (Kieschnick 2003: 71).

Second is the extent of destruction during the Cultural Revolution, which in turn is connected to how the story of this movement has been presented, both within China and abroad. The Communist Party has portrayed this period as *shi nian haojie*, "the ten years of catastrophe," which has sometimes been equated with a cultural holocaust in foreign language publications (Gao 2008: 15). In addition, the majority of memoirs, biographies, and autobiographies that describe this period have been written by former Party members and elites who suffered or former Red Guards who regret their actions. Books such as Jung Chang's *Wild Swans* (2003), Nien Cheng's *Life and Death in Shanghai* (1987), and Gao Yuan's *Born Red* (1987) emphasize an atmosphere of mass paranoia and chaos and a breakdown of social order. Because the dominant narrative of the Cultural Revolution has been shaped by its targets, the received wisdom is that the entire movement was an unmitigated disaster that set China back decades in its development efforts and created a lost generation. Yet, as Gao Mobo argues, if this campaign is analyzed from a socioeconomic class perspective, its effects and outcomes are more complicated. Gao, himself a former Red Guard, argues that after political stability was restored in 1969, the Cultural Revolution had many positive effects, such as new infrastructure, improved education and health care in rural areas, and markedly increased production in rural enterprises (Gao 2008: 5).

The actual impact on cultural heritage is equally complicated. Mao's "four olds" campaign (against ideas, customs, culture, and habits) was launched in August 1966, peaked the following month, and was largely abandoned by late 1967. During this campaign, students and youth were encouraged to attack and eradicate all evidence of "old thinking" and "old culture." Most of the destruction and killing that followed was aimed at individuals and their private collections. Indeed, the fact that the State Administration for Cultural Heritage has estimated that China currently has more than 400,000 current heritage sites demonstrates the extent to which the "four olds" campaign failed to eradicate the country's public heritage. Desecration, not outright destruction, became the order of the day.

In fact, state cultural holdings appear to have *increased* during the Cultural Revolution, especially after March 1967, when the State Council, Central Military Commission, and Party Central Committee issued a joint decree ordering Red Guards to protect all state property, including cultural relics. Objects and books seized from private homes were directed away from paper mills and smelting plants to state warehouses, museums, and libraries, where they could be categorized and stored (Ho 2006: 69–71).

While premier Zhou Enlai has been widely credited in China for protecting the country's most important heritage sites against destruction during this era, he clearly did not act alone. Indeed, just as the "Gang of Four"[2] has been blamed for all of the negative consequences of the entire Cultural Revolution, Zhou has been solely credited for all of the positive outcomes, such as cultural protection. He did not, however, act alone. At the national level, the protection of material culture and heritage sites was defended by some Party leaders as necessary in order to teach the masses about China's feudal past, while for others, this was an excuse for personal enrichment. At the local level, a combination of civic pride, suspicion of outsiders, and an authentic desire to preserve the past motivated both state and non-state actors (Ho 2006). Finally, this campaign against the past paradoxically required not the forgetting of this but its remembrance. As Rubie Watson has noted, "that which was to be forgotten had to be attacked; to be attacked it had to be remembered – it follows, therefore, that in forgetting "the legacy" was revived, if only as a negative example" (1995:14).

In summary, widespread material destruction was the norm for approximately one year, between mid-1966 and late 1967. This was spurred by the iconoclasm of the Cultural Revolution and demonstrated its (albeit extreme) links with the century-long modernization movement in China that began with Sun Yat-sen's attack on Qing rulers as foreign occupiers before the 1911 Revolution, continued with the New Culture Movement's critique of Chinese traditions beginning in 1919 and the KMT's early attacks on Confucianism in the 1920s, and reached its logical conclusion with Mao's call to youth to "smash the old" in August 1966. For example, the historian Gu Jiegang (1895–1980), writing in 1926, called for the careful investigation of "spurious works" and "unauthenticated history" (quoted in De Bary and Lufrano 2000: 364), while Hu Shi (1891–1962), who studied under the American philosopher John Dewey at Columbia University, advocated a philosophy of life based on science (ibid, 375–377). Similarly, a Nationalist Party decree issued in February 1927 described Confucianism as "superstitious and out of place in the modern world" and called for the destruction of Confucian temples (Li 1987: 17).

These examples show how traditional practices and, by implication heritage, being fundamentally conservative, have been attacked by modernizers of all political persuasions in China, not just Marxists. What makes the current politics of China different is the fact that cultural practices and materials have been redefined as resources under the guise of first development and more recently sustainability (Winter and Daly 2011: 19). This process has opened up the realm of culture to capital accumulation, accentuating class differences. Nothing more graphically demonstrates this class factor than the ticket prices for China's most

---

[2] 'The Gang of Four' is the named used by the Communist Party to describe four key leaders who, after Mao's death in 1976, were blamed for the chaos of the Cultural Revolution. These were Jiang Qing, Mao's wife; Zhang Chunqiao, second deputy premier; Yao Wenyuan, a member of the Party's Politburo; and Wang Hongwen, who was Vice-Chairman of the Politburo at the time of his arrest. Jiang Qing and Zhang were each sentenced to death (commuted to life imprisonment in 1983), Yao to 20 years, and Wang to life imprisonment. Jiang subsequently committed suicide while on medical release in 1991. Zhang was paroled in 1998 and died of cancer in 2005. Yao was released from prison in 1996 and died of diabetes, also in 2005. Wang Hongwen was never released, and died of liver cancer in 1992.

famous heritage sites. Indeed, the use of prohibitive admission fees as a way of controlling visitor arrivals and thereby helping preserve key heritage sites might well in the near future mean the transformation of cultural tourism in China into a class activity, much like golf (see Chap. 5).

The most lasting damage of the Cultural Revolution was to education and what in Chinese is called public morality (*gongde*). All schooling was halted for several years, and when universities reopened, history, literature, and other subjects deemed to be "bourgeois" were banned. In 1969, teams of workers were placed in charge of higher education institutions, effectively ending formal education for a generation. Besides an enormous waste of human potential, these policies did significant damage to society's collective memory of the past. This fact, combined with the wrenching political shifts that saw the Communist Party under Mao turn on itself only to repudiate Maoism and embrace market reforms under Deng Xiaoping, has left a significant moral quandary. The Communist Party today has largely abandoned communism; it justifies its rule on its delivery of consistent economic growth, the maintenance of public order, and citizens' right to increase their personal wealth. The question is how sustainable this model is in a society in which faith (be this in communism or religion) has been shattered. The net result is that heritage sites, museums, and artifacts now serve political *and* pedagogical purposes. If some sites foreground cultural nationalist propaganda, others aim to educate visitors about their own collective past. Tourism has a key role in this pedagogical effort; from the state perspective, cultural tourism is a means of reconstituting "a shared cultural grammar" (Nyiri 2006: 12).

Consequently, the beginning of the reform period in 1979 saw a significant shift in how the Party and state viewed the past. In 1982, the country's first *Law on the Protection of Cultural Heritage of the People's Republic of China* was issued by the State Council. They also issued an expanded list of national protected sites. Numbering 242, these included 43 revolutionary sites, 19 grottoes, 13 stone carvings, 26 tombs, 105 buildings, and 36 ancient sites (Liu 1983: 97). The Chinese government also ratified the World Heritage Convention in 1985 and, a few years later, made cultural heritage preservation a part of its national 5-year plans. The 1982 law, which remains the basis of heritage policies in China, established guidelines for the categorization of heritage, excavation procedures, and site protection. In doing so, it explicitly linked cultural preservation with the political objectives of nationalism, socialism, and modernization (Sofield and Li 1998: 370–371). In other words, preserving the past was not defined as an end in itself; this should instead serve to encourage a national consciousness, reflect socialist values, and aid with material development in the present.

China's first world heritage sites, inscribed in 1987, included the Great Wall, Beijing's Forbidden City and the nearby Peking Man archeological site at Zhoukoudian, the Mausoleum of Qin Shi Huangdi outside of Xian, and Mount Tai (*Taishan*), an imperial pilgrimage site for more than 2,000 years. These are all sites that a generation before had been either physically attacked or harshly critiqued as feudal remnants. Historical sites such as these, and by extension tourism, soon came to be viewed as economic resources which could contribute to the modernization of

China, build patriotism, and provide people with a sense of the Party's historical interpretation. A striking example of this was the extensive renovation of the Potala Palace in Lhasa carried out beginning in 1989 and its subsequent inscription on UNESCO's world heritage list in 1994. This transformation of the Dalai Lama's former center of power into a national and world heritage site was funded by the same government that had led a three-decade-long campaign against Tibetan culture, religion, and sovereignty claims. Upon completion of this project, the Potala opened to the public as a heritage museum (Sofield and Li 1998: 375).

The 1982 law also introduced the concept of "heritage" (*yichan*). It established the National Cultural Administrative Bureau (renamed the State Administration of Cultural Heritage in 1988) as well as state conservation organizations at provincial, municipal, and local levels.[3] In addition, it also established an expanded system for classifying cultural sites. However, funding and implementing heritage projects was largely left to local authorities, a critical issue we will return to in Chap. 5.

In the last two decades, heritage has become a key component of China's booming tourism industry but is still defined as a political project by national authorities. The Communist Party-led campaign to embrace modernization through the rhetoric of market capitalism has led to an ideological crisis. If communism and socialism are shunted aside, what will serve as the basis of continued Party rule? More specifically, in presenting its own past, how can the CCP reconcile a revolutionary message of self-sacrifice with its contemporary advocacy of self-interest in a "decidedly unrevolutionary present" (Denton 2005: 581)?

As the Party has shifted away from a Maoist emphasis on class struggle, it has promoted a carefully controlled nationalism as one answer to this dilemma (Lee 2008). Thus, the CCP's revolutionary narrative is now linked to a patriotic narrative in the display and presentation of heritage (Svensson 2006: 7). This can be seen, for example, in the official depiction of the Sino-Japanese War, which lasted from 1937 to Japan's defeat at the end of the Second World War. In an analysis of war museums in Beijing, Shenyang, and Nanjing,[4] Rana Mitter (2005) shows how in each of these memorial spaces the Republican government has been reconfigured from anticommunist villains to flawed patriots in the fight against Japan. No longer is the official narrative a story of liberation from an oppressive military regime and an overthrow of the bourgeois class; instead, it is a story of a collective national struggle against a foreign invader. According to this new narrative, the KMT and its supporters were not inherently bad; they were simply on the wrong side of history, even if they tried to fight the good fight.

Since 1949, museums have served as a primary medium for communicating and promoting state and Party perspectives. Between 1949 and 1979, all museums, whatever their focus, faithfully followed a historical materialist framework that depicted

---

[3] These were called provincial [*shengji*], municipal [*shiji*], and county [*xianji*] "cultural relic protection work units" [*wenwu baohu danwei*].

[4] The Memorial Museum of the People's War of Resistance against Japan in Beijing, the September 18th Memorial Museum in Shenyang, and the Museum of the Nanjing Massacre in Nanjing

the present as liberation from an exploitative past and ended their narratives with popular resistance and collective struggle. In an era of Communist Party-directed market reforms and an official emphasis on individual effort and initiative, the former museum emphasis on collective sacrifice has not been abandoned, it has been enlarged upon. Patriotism, national unity, and a strong China standing up to take its place in the world have become crucial components of this new narrative. The newly renovated and recently reopened National Museum of China in Tiananmen Square in Beijing reflects this message. The museum has two permanent halls, "Ancient China," covering the Paleolithic era to the Qing Dynasty, and "the Road to Rejuvenation," covering the final decades of the Qing, the Republican era, and the People's Republic. The "Ancient China" hall is organized chronologically and follows a historical materialist pattern, tracing the progressive development of new forms of technology and social organization. However, the previous emphasis on interpreting the past through the universal stages mapped out by Engels and Morgan has been eliminated. Instead, visitors are able to see the emergence of new forms of material culture (from pottery and bronzes to iron, steel, and glazed pottery) as well as the development of more complex and intricate designs and patterns. One of the only politically explicit messages in this hall is a consistent emphasis on national unity. For example, in introducing the Spring and Autumn period (722–403 BCE), curators briefly discuss the variety of ethnic groups that inhabited the central plains at the time, note that these groups began to interact during this period, and conclude that this "laid the foundation for a unified multiethnic country." Similarly, after noting the fragmentation of political authority that followed the collapse of the Eastern Han Dynasty (25 BCE-220 AD), a placard declares, "There was unprecedented national interaction during this period, laying the foundation for a unified multiethnic country in the subsequent Sui and Tang Dynasties." The actual independence of frontier peoples during the Sui (581–618 AD) and Tang is then noted but is credited to the "open ethnic policy" of the state. Moreover, what has become a familiar claim – that non-Han peoples learned from the Han – is here introduced (Fig. 3.2):

> Frontier peoples learned from the economic and cultural achievements of the Han people and at the same time became an important cultural influence contributing to Han lifestyle and culture. Despite occasional conflicts, ethnic integration continued to strengthen the unified China as a multi-ethnic country.

This claim situates not just "the Han people" in an era (the Tang Dynasty) when empirical evidence for any such identity label does not exist but also does the same for ethnic groups such as the Uighurs, despite widespread scientific agreement that no such collective identity marker existed in present-day Xinjiang until the nineteenth century (Sautman 2001). It thus takes a pressing contemporary political issue and seeks to locate this in a claimed shared historical past.

The "Ancient China" hall ends with a glossed-over description of technological and territorial advances during Qing rule (1644–1911). Left unmentioned are the Manchurian origins of the Qing Dynasty or their emphasis on distinguishing themselves from their subject peoples through dress, hair style, and spatial segregation. Instead, they are depicted as Chinese. Even more remarkably, the "Road to

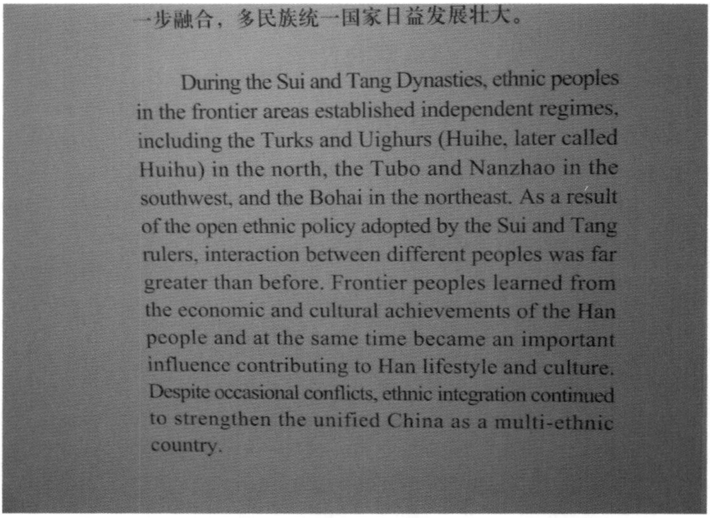

一步融合，多民族统一国家日益发展壮大。

During the Sui and Tang Dynasties, ethnic peoples
in the frontier areas established independent regimes,
including the Turks and Uighurs (Huihe, later called
Huihu) in the north, the Tubo and Nanzhao in the
southwest, and the Bohai in the northeast. As a result
of the open ethnic policy adopted by the Sui and Tang
rulers, interaction between different peoples was far
greater than before. Frontier peoples learned from
the economic and cultural achievements of the Han
people and at the same time became an important
influence contributing to Han lifestyle and culture.
Despite occasional conflicts, ethnic integration continued
to strengthen the unified China as a multi-ethnic
country.

Fig. 3.2 Imagining a multiethnic historic China: interpretive panel, National Museum of China, Beijing

Rejuvenation" hall begins not with the rise of the Communist Party but a description of nineteenth-century foreign encroachments and attempts by members of the Qing regime to resist. The standard Nationalist Party narrative of the Qing as a foreign occupier and Communist Party narrative of them as a feudal regime has been largely erased, replaced with an emphasis on the patriotic motives of all Chinese (including members of the ruling class) who resisted attacks against China. This focus on patriotism and national unity dominates the entire exhibit. Neither the Qing nor the Nationalists are portrayed as enemies of the people, feudal oppressors, or lackeys of foreigners; instead, both regimes are depicted as containing elements of patriotic resistance. However, ultimate success (redefined as national unification, not as a class-based victory for socialism) is depicted as only having been achieved under the leadership of the Communist Party. Indeed, other than a single set of portraits of Marx and Engels, the place of Marxism in China's twentieth-century history is largely downplayed (Fig. 3.3).

This emphasis on national unity under the leadership of the Communist Party is also the dominant theme in newly opened or renovated provincial museums. For example, in an exhibit on the war against Japan in the recently renovated Inner Mongolian Museum in Hohhot, class struggle and feudal oppression are completely absent, replaced by a shared struggle of Mongolians and Han Chinese against invasion:

> After the Opium War ended in 1840, imperialist countries like Japan and Russia etc. sped up their steps to dismember Inner Mongolia. The half-century successively by Qing Dynasty (1644–1911), Northern Warlord government (1911–1927) and Kuomintang Government (1927–1949) made the people of different ethnic groups in Inner Mongolia live a miserable

Fig. 3.3 Diorama of nationalist revolutionaries attacking Qing forces in 1911 (National Museum of China, Beijing)

life in a semi-colonial and semi-feudal society. This was worsened after Japan's gradual invasion starting from September 18, 1931. In order to fight against the imperialist invasion and the feudal rule, people in Inner Mongolia had had a long –term continuous struggle … historical experiences show that only the Chinese Communist Party, which had experienced the long-term revolution and practice, can issue a policy to meet the needs of Mongols and the situations in the Inner Mongolia Autonomous Region. The Chinese Communist Party can lead Mongols in the right way to liberation and freedom. The founding of the Inner Mongolia Government was a successful example of the regional autonomy policy of the Chinese Communist Party (Introduction, "Beacon Fire on the Grassland" exhibit, Inner Mongolian Provincial Museum, 2008).

Notably absent in both the Inner Mongolian and National Museums' twentieth-century exhibits are large numbers of material objects. Instead, curators rely on still and video images, dioramas, and multimedia technology to tell their stories of patriotism. But the reliance on images in the "Road to Rejuvenation" exhibit as compared to an emphasis on tangible objects in the "Ancient China" exhibit is not indicative of a curatorial turn to postmodernist play or cool irony. That is to say, this is not a sign of a message that cannot be told or a history that cannot be displayed, but a tool to attract a (domestic) audience at a time in which mass consumption has become the overriding ideological message (Denton 2005: 577). This shift away from straightforward propaganda to a visitor-friendly message does not, therefore, mean a shift away from an explicit focus on a central political message. Far from being an embrace of endlessly possible interpretations, the intent in both exhibits is a clear story line (Fig. 3.4).

Fig. 3.4 "Fire on the Grasslands": war against Japan exhibit, Inner Mongolia Museum, Hohhot, 2009

The "Road to Rejuvenation" exhibit closes with a placard entitled "Afterword," a new call to arms:

We shall closely unite around the CPC central leadership with Hu Jintao as its General Secretary, hold high the great banner of socialism with Chinese characteristics, follow the guidance of Marxist-Leninism, Mao Zedong Thought, Deng Xiaoping Theory and the Important Thought of 'Three Represents', carry out the Scientific Outlook on Development thoroughly, join efforts to forge ahead and persistently strive for the great goals of implementing the 12th Five-Year Program and building a moderately prosperous society (National Museum of China, June 2012).

Taken seriously, this political evocation is riddled with contradictions, from the oxymoronic basis of "Marxist-Leninism" to the fundamental differences between Maoist aspirations for transcending Marxist historical stages of material and social development and Deng Xiaoping's advocacy of market-driven production and individual wealth. Yet its conclusion with a call for "moderate prosperity" also signifies the Party's rejection of, ironically, communism. A former ideological focus on revolution and class struggle has been replaced by a nationalist and sentimentalist look back, a form of nostalgia that rejects an empirically driven depiction of the recent past as effectively as did the previous revolutionary narrative.

This new narrative of what might be termed market-driven development with patriotic characteristics and an increasingly nonmaterial interpretation of the past is increasingly widespread in contemporary China. Besides museums, this message is also part of the construction of Ming-, Qing-, and Republican-era "old towns" in various Chinese cities, ranging in size from a single street (such as a Republican-era "snack street" off of Beijing's Wangfujing pedestrian shopping area) to an entire quarter (such as Shanghai's Xintiandi quarter, a bustling enclave of designer boutiques and trendy bars in a former working-class neighborhood). These typically combine newly built "authentic" buildings with service workers in period costumes. The recently completed reconstruction of Beijing's Qianmen neighborhood, west of Tiananmen Square, is a good example. In the 1950s, this area became home to a new working class, its hundreds of courtyard homes divided into small apartments. These have in turn been demolished and replaced with a newly built "old" Qianmen district, complete with buildings deigned to mimic the built space of the late nineteenth and early twentieth century, along with a retro-tram line (that goes nowhere). One of the ironies of this project is the fact that the Beijing government demolished postliberation development (workers' housing) to recreate built space as it had been in "feudal" China, albeit devoid of authentic signifiers such as beggars, opium smokers, gangsters, prostitutes, or warlord soldiers.

As part of this patriotic-nationalism campaign, state authorities emphasize China's multiethnic but unified cultural landscape. For example, Article One of the State Administration for Cultural Heritage's (SACH) "Principles for the Conservation of Heritage Sites in China" declares that China is a unified country "with an unbroken cultural tradition" and the purpose of heritage conservation is to "strengthen national unity and promote sustainable development of the national culture" (Agnew and Demas 2004: 59). This reflects the more than century-long campaign to cultivate a national conscious among Chinese, with roots in the pre-1911 revolutionary movement led by Sun Yat-sen, regarded in both China and Taiwan as the Father (*guofu*) of modern China.

While there is widespread disagreement about the outcomes of various state policies during both the Republic era (1911–1949) and after 1949, it is difficult to argue with the success of this national identity campaign. Indeed, the biological basis of Han identity and the leadership role of Han people are now taken as natural by the vast majority of PRC citizens who self-identify as Han. In this sense, Sun Yat-sen's racial nationalism has trumped both Marxism and Maoism and is reflected not just in popular culture but also in the scientific record, such as in paleoanthropology.

At a time at which the global scientific community has rejected race as a biological category, paleoanthropology in the People's Republic has claimed this as in fact factually valid.

For example, there is widespread agreement within the international scientific community with the "Out of Africa" hypothesis of human origins, which theorizes that *Homo sapiens* emerged approximately 143,000 years ago in Eastern Africa and subsequently spread around the world, eventually displacing *Homo erectus*. Yet both mainstream paleoanthropological opinion and state authorities in China reject this view, arguing that human remains found at Zhoukoudian outside Beijing and known as Peking Man are evidence of not just a "Chinese race" (*zhonghua minzu*) but of a "yellow race," the ancestors of all East Asians (Sautman 2001: 96). This is in spite of the fact that Peking Man was not a *Homo sapien* but a *Homo erectus* and has been dated to 500,000 years ago. The official Chinese explanation of this discrepancy is that *Homo sapiens* emerged in different places and at different times. In other words, rather than common human ancestors spreading out from Africa, a unique "Chinese race" has its roots in its own unique ancestor(s). While this claim could be dismissed as a nationalist myth or as a state attempt to trump scientifically based ethnomorphosis with politically inspired ethnogenesis, it is important to note the racial nationalist basis of this argument, which is very different than the current civic nationalism that predominates in the world (Sautman 2001: 108). Not only does the Chinese government assert that contemporary China is heir to an unbroken civilization that dates back to 3,000 BCE but also that contemporary Han Chinese are biologically the same as their putative distant ancestors.

One response to this is to note that current policies in China are actually no different than previous nation-building policies in most of Europe and North America in the past. In this sense, China is not different; it has simply begun this process later (Kohl 1998: 226). This, however, ignores the overwhelming scientific evidence against both the scientific basis of "race" and the claim that a unified Chinese civilization has existed for 5,000 years.

Although a racial nationalist campaign has succeeded among the majority of (Han) Chinese citizens, in minority areas of the PRC, the situation is quite different. A striking example is the saga of the "Xinjiang mummies." Shortly after the end of the Cultural Revolution, Chinese archeologists led by Wang Binghua uncovered more than 100 well-preserved corpses in the Tarim Basin, a vast desert region in Xinjiang, some dating back to 2,000 BCE. At the main site of Qizilchoqa, east of the city of Ürümqi, 113 mummies were found, all of which date to 1,200 BCE. These findings are significant for two reasons: all of the mummies found to date are not of nobility but common people, providing invaluable insight into everyday life thousands of years ago, and all of these mummies have Caucasoid features (Hadingham 1994). DNA testing carried out in 2004 provided scientific evidence of non-East Asian origins, which raises questions not just about the dominant Chinese narrative of Chinese civilization but also about Chinese territorial claims. Indeed, Uyghur separatists have claimed these early settlers as their ancestors and asserted these mummies prove Xinjiang was never Chinese until quite recently. Yet DNA testing has also demonstrated that the biological ancestors of today's Uyghur communities arrived in the Tarim region from Mongolia in the ninth century CE, more than 2,000 years *after* these mummies were buried (Thurbon 2011; Hare 2009). The political sensitivity of these Indo-European artifacts led to the abrupt curtailment of an exhibit at the University of Pennsylvania in 2011 when the State Administration of Cultural Heritage ordered that all but three mummies be returned to China in the middle of the exhibit (Rothstein 2011).

This conflict over the public display abroad of the human remains of people who clearly were neither Chinese nor Uyghur demonstrates the underlying political issues involved in heritage conservation. This also serves as a reminder that the promotion of heritage tourism in minority areas is allowed in China only so long as this does not, from the state view, threaten national unity. What is conserved and displayed must be presented as an example of a national (Chinese) consciousness (Shepherd 2006, 2008). This example also shows how there actually is no multicultural state policy in China. The official government position is that the word *minzu* was mistakenly translated as "nationality" by early revolutionaries, when it should only have meant "ethnicity" (Zhang Qian 2010). Yet the Party itself translated the *Guojia Minzu Shiwu Weiyuanhui* as the "State Commission for Nationality Affairs" until 1995, when this was retranslated as the "State Commission for Ethnic Affairs" and the catch phrase *minzu tuanjie* was changed in English from "the unity of nationalities" to "ethnic unity" (Zhang Haiyang 1997: 79; Gladney 2004). Evoking Confucius, authorities now argue that China for thousands of years has been a nation of many ethnic groups, all linked by a shared culture. In other words (and correctly, from a Confucian perspective), all the various peoples who came into contact with the Middle Kingdom could become "Chinese," regardless of race or ethnicity, by embracing Confucian cultural pillars. However, according to this new official position, early revolutionaries mistakenly framed this culture issue in the language of nationhood, borrowed from the dominant rhetoric of late nineteenth-century European imperialism.

To be Chinese, then, from the official perspective of the Communist Party, is to accept the core principles of Chinese culture, no longer defined by the five relationships and three bonds of Confucianism[5] but by the language of socialist modernization. At the heart of this narrative is a key assumption about culture, namely, that an authentic Chinese identity requires people to transcend and overcome what they may think of as their own *ethnos* or culture, in the sense of customs, habits, norms, and values. This means that a Tibetan, Mongolian, or other minority citizen becomes Chinese by learning to speak Chinese and presumably practicing the normative values of the (Han) Chinese majority. Hence, this is not a multicultural policy, which demands respect and toleration for cultural differences, because such an acceptance would undermine the logic of the state perspective. At best, it is a multi*ethnic* policy that cultivates superficial differences. To be simultaneously different and Chinese,

---

[5] The five Confucian relationships define how people should interact and are premised on the fundamental inequality of society. These relations are ruler and subject, father and son, elder brother and younger brother, husband and wife, and (the only human bond based on equal standing) friend to friend.

an official ethnic minority can only be different at a surface level, such as in appearance, language, music, and dance; she must be the same as a Han Chinese in mental outlook and her thinking about the world.

This means in practice an ongoing state attempt to capture the tangible symbols of cultural differences and refurbish these as elements in a national project of unity. Thus, the Potala Palace in Lhasa, the former home of the Dalai Lama and a World Heritage site, is described in application documents for UNESCO status as an example of Tibetan and Han Chinese cooperation, while the town of Lijiang in Yunnan Province, formerly the center of Naxi social and political life, was nominated for world heritage status based on its "harmonious fusion of different cultural traditions" (UNESCO 1997). This emphasis on cooperation among different ethnic groups is the dominant theme in applications for international status for heritage sites in minority regions. Even the former Qing imperial summer resort at Chengde, north of Beijing, has been reinterpreted to support this claim despite the fact that it was designed as a place where the Manchurian ruling elite could be free of (Han) Chinese influence to interact with other (non-Chinese) peoples such as Tibetans and Mongolians. Yet the state application for world heritage status for this site emphasizes its historical importance in promoting "national unity" (Hevia 2001: 224). This is similar to how the archeological site at Xanadu, the Mongolian capital established by Kublai Khan in 1256, is described in its inscription on the world heritage list, as important because it, "exhibits a unique attempt to assimilate the nomadic Mongolian and Han Chinese cultures" (UNESCO World Heritage List, 2012). Similarly, a common stop on China Travel Service (CTS) tours is the tomb of Zhaojun near Hohhot, the capital of Inner Mongolia. This memorial site commemorates Wang Zhaojun, a Chinese woman who married a *Chanyu* (leader) of the nomadic Xiongnu people during the Han Dynasty (220 BCE-220 CE). Although this is not the actual, burial place of Wang, the site has been significantly improved for tourism in recent years and touted as evidence of ethnic cooperation in China (Fig. 3.5).

Branding and selling minority culture and heritage is not limited to the Chinese state. It is important to acknowledge, for example, the increasing number of Tibetan entrepreneurs in places as far flung as Lhasa, Zhongdian (Yunnan), Xiahe (Gansu), Kangding (Sichuan), Mount Wutai (Shanxi), and even Beijing and Shanghai who have sought to capitalize on a growing Han Chinese infatuation with Tibet to open hotels, restaurants, jewelry stores, and art shops.

Moreover, the Tibetan government in exile has publicly supported tourism in Tibetan areas as a development tool. A 2007 report on development and the environment in Tibet argued that the total volume of tourism in Tibet is not a problem but the fact that the vast majority of visitors go only to the Lhasa valley (GOT 2007: 192–193). The authors of this report argued for an increased focus on ecotourism in rural communities. This would, they suggested, further development in isolated communities, reduce tourism pressures in Lhasa, and provide visitors with a more authentic Tibetan experience. However, the authors of this report take as a fact (that tourism is primarily "Western") what in actuality is a fiction: the percentage of European and American tourists in the TAR is largely insignificant. Thus, a focus on improving the English language capacities of tour guides (189) and meeting the

Fig. 3.5 Tomb of Wang Zhaojun (first century BCE), one of China's "Four Ancient Beauties," near Hohhot, Inner Mongolia

expectations of Western visitors (194) is oddly out of place, given the realities of the tourism industry in the TAR.

Finally, as we discuss in Chap. 4, the promotion of domestic tourism as a by-product of heritage preservation has been linked by the national government to the development of "higher-quality" citizens with a "civilized" (*wenming*) consciousness (Chio 2010) (Fig. 3.6). Established by the State Council in 2006, the China Central Spiritual Civilization Steering Committee has been tasked by the State Council with molding "civilized" modern subjects. While often critiqued and even ridiculed by outside observers, this "quality" campaign reflects deep cultural assumptions about the public role of Confucian subjects as well as Chinese perspectives on a materialist approach to both history and economic development. To be specific, modernization is viewed by CCP authorities as both a material and spiritual/mental project. This is at once a Party response to assumptions about the close ties between modernization and "Westernization" held by globalization advocates, to its own legacy as a Marxist political movement, and to practical concerns about public behavior, environmental problems, and the Maoist abuse of nature.

In summary, heritage destinations such as museums, national memorials, archeological sites, and historic built space have an explicit public education purpose, which is still shaped by the Communist Party. But unlike the "patriotic education bases" of the pre-Cultural Revolution, contemporary heritage sites are not limited to

Fig. 3.6 The state protects history? Signs such as these are common at Chinese heritage sites

sanitized Maoist and Stalinist interpretations. Given the expanded mobility, incomes, and entertainment choices of many Chinese citizens, Party authorities and by extension local state actors must grapple with how the past is presented in a post-Maoist era and how to attract an audience.

Ultimately the Party seeks to maintain control of how history is interpreted, which simply cannot be reconciled with a rigorous critical analysis. But what cannot so easily be controlled in a consumer-driven market economy is oral history, the stuff of intangible heritage. Thus, although recent political events such as the Cultural Revolution and the Tiananmen Square movement have been eliminated from the state historical narrative, these are being remembered through ongoing, non-state oral history projects. These projects aim to document a peoples' memory (*mingjian*) in place of material archives that are restricted (Bonnin 2007: 59). This attempt to use the intangibles of collective memory as a counterpoint to a state project of amnesia demonstrates the underlying political basis of heritage.

Bibliography

Agnew, Neville, and Martha Demas (eds.). 2004. *Principles for the conservation of heritage in China*. Los Angeles: The Getty Conservatory Institute.

Bai, Liu. 1983. *Cultural policy in the People's Republic of China: Letting a hundred flowers bloom*. Paris: UNESCO.

Bonnin, Michel. 2007. The threatened history and collective memory of the cultural revolution's lost generation. *China Perspectives* 4: 52–64.

Chang, Jung. 2003. Wild Swans: Three Daughters of China. New York: Simon & Schuster.

Cheng, Nien. 1987. Life and Death in Shanghai. New York: Flamingo Press.

Chio, Jenny. 2010. China's campaign for civilized tourism: What to do when tourists behave badly. *Anthropology News* 51(8): 14–15.

De Bary, Theodore, and Richard Lufrano (eds.). 2000. *Sources of Chinese tradition*, vol. II. New York: Columbia University Press.

Denton, Kirk. 2005. Museums, memorial sites and exhibitionary culture in the People's Republic of China. *China Quarterly* 183(September): 565–586.

Dikőtter, Frank. 1992. *The discourse of race in modern China*. Palo Alto: Stanford University Press.

Dikőtter, Frank. 2010. *Mao's great famine: The history of China's most devastating catastrophe, 1958–1962*. New York: Walker.

Fowler, Don. 1987. "Uses of the Past: Archeology in the Service of the State." American Antiquity 52(2): 229–248.

Gao Yuan, 1987. Born Red: A Chronicle of the Cultural Revolution. Palo Alto, CA: Stanford University Press.

Gladney, Dru. 2004. *Dislocating China: Reflections on Muslims, minorities and other subaltern subjects*. Chicago: University of Chicago.

Government of Tibet, Department of Information and International Relations. Central Tibetan Administration. 2007. *Tibet: A human development and environmental report*. Dharamsala: Government of Tibet.

Hadingham, Evan. 1994. The mummies of Xinjiang. *Discover* Magazine, April. http://discovermagazine. com/1994/apr/themummiesofxinj359/. Accessed 12 July 2012.

Haiyan, Lee. 2008. The ruins of *Yuangmingyuan* or, how to enjoy a national wound. *Modern China* 20(10): 1–36.

Hare, John. 2009. The mysteries of the Gobi desert. *Asian Affairs* 40(3): 408–417.

Hevia, James. 2001. World heritage, national culture, and the restoration of Chengde. *Positions* 9(1): 219–243.

Ho, David Dahpon. 2006. To protect and preserve: Resisting the destroy the four olds campaign, 1966–1967. In *The Chinese cultural revolution as history*, ed. Joseph Esherick et al. Palo Alto: Stanford University Press.

Hung, Wu. 2005. *Remaking Beijing: Tiananmen Square and the creation of a public space*. Chicago: University of Chicago.

Keightley, David N. 1977. Archeology and history in China. In *Paleoanthropology in the People's Republic of China*, ed. W.W. Howells and Patricia Jones Tsuchitani. Washington, DC: National Academy of Sciences.

Kieschnick, John. 2003. *The impact of Buddhism on Chinese material culture*. Princeton, NJ: Princeton University Press.

Kohl, Philip. 1998. Nationalism and archeology. *Annual Review of Anthropology* 27: 233–246.

Li Jinyu. 1987. The politics of propriety: A comparative study of the new life movement and the five stresses and four beautifications campaign in twentieth century China. Masters' thesis. Houston: Rice University.

Logan, William. 2007. Closing Pandora's box: Human rights conundrums in cultural heritage protection. In *Cultural heritage and human rights*, ed. Silverman Helaine and D. Fairchild Ruggles, 33–52. New York: Springer.

Min, Zhuang. 1989. The administration of China's archeological heritage. In *Archeological heritage management in the modern world*, ed. Henry Cleere, 102–109. Oxford: Unwin Hyman.

Mitter, Rita. 2005. Educating citizens through war museums in modern China. In *Manufacturing citizenship: Education and nationalism in Europe, Asia, and China*, ed. Benei Veronique, 129–142. London: Routledge.

Mobo, Gao. 2008. *The battle for China's past: Mao and the cultural revolution*. London: Pluto Press.

National Museum of China. June 2012. "Road to Rejuvenation" Exhibit, Beijing, China.

Nyiri, Pal. 2006. *Scenic spots: Chinese tourism, the state, and cultural authority*. Seattle: University of Washington.

Qian, Zhang. 2010. *China's ethnic groups and religion*. Beijing: China International Press.

Rothstein, Edward. 2011. Another stop on a long, improbable journey. The *New York Times*, February21.http://www.nytimes.com/2011/02/21/arts/design/21silk.html?_r=1&pagewanted=all. Accessed 12 July 2012.

Shepherd, Robert. 2006. UNESCO and the politics of cultural heritage in Tibet. *Journal of Contemporary Asia* 36(2): 243–257.

Shepherd, Robert. 2008. Cultural heritage, UNESCO, and the Chinese state: Whose heritage and for whom? *Heritage Management* 2(1): 55–79.

Sautman, Barry. 2001. Peking man and the politics of paleoanthropological nationalism in China. *Journal of Asian Studies* 60(1): 95–124.

Sofield, Trevor, and Fung Mei Li. 1998. Tourism development and cultural policies in China. *Annals of Tourism Research* 25(2): 362–392.

Svensson, Marina. 2006. *In the ancestor's shadow: Cultural heritage contestations in Chinese Villages*. Working paper #16. Stockholm: Centre for East and Southeast Asian Studies, Lund University.

Thurbon, Colin. 2011. The secrets of the mummies. *The New York Review of Books*, May 12. http://www.nybooks.com/articles/archives/2011/may/12/secrets-mummies/. Accessed 12 July 2012.

Tong, Fanzheng. 1995. Thirty years of Chinese archeology. In *Nationalism, politics and the practice of archeology*, ed. Philip Kohl and Hawcett Clare. Cambridge: Cambridge University Press.

United Nations Educational, Scientific, and Cultural Organization. 1997. *World heritage committee, twenty-first session*. Naples, 1–6 Dec 1997. http://whc.unesco.org/archive/1997/whc-97-conf208-10reve.pdf. Accessed 2 May 2012.

UNESCO. 2003. *Convention for the safeguarding of intangible cultural heritage*. Electronic document. http://www.unesco.org/culture/ich/index.php?pg=00006. Accessed 28 June 2012.

UNESCO. 2012. *World heritage list: Xanadu*. Paris: United Nations Educational, Scientific, and Cultural Organization. http://whc.unesco.org/en/list/1389. Accessed 9 July 2012.

Watson, Rubie. 1995. Palaces, museums, squares: Chinese national spaces. *Museum Anthropology* 19(2): 7–19.

Winter, Tim, and Patrick Daly. 2011. Heritage in Asia: Converging forces, conflicting values. In *Routledge handbook of heritage in Asia*, ed. Patrick Daly and Tim Winter, 1–35. London: Routledge Press.

Zhang Haiyang. 1997. Wrestling with the connotations of Chinese 'Minzu'. *Economic and Political Weekly*, July 26, pp. 74–84.

Chapter 4
Nature, Culture, and Civilization

This chapter explores underlying differences between Euro-American and Chinese perspectives on preservation and heritage management. Assumptions about the relationship of "nature" to "culture" and the rationale for material preservation are, in the case of China, quite complex, combining Confucian and Daoist perspectives on the place of humans within nature, a traditional Buddhist lack of concern for material preservation, and a hypermodernizing, broadly utilitarian Maoist-derived emphasis on material growth at the expense of the past and a subsequent exploitation of natural resources. This emphasis on growth has only recently begun to be questioned, as seen for example in an emerging environmental movement in China and a state shift at the national level toward environmental stewardship and sustainable development initiatives.

Any discussion of environmental and cultural protection has to take place within the context of globalization. At the most basic level, this process is claimed to be contesting and erasing cultural, social, economic, and political differences within and between societies. The net result will be, depending on one's view, a world of bleak sameness and cultural monotony or a world of individual agency freed of the barriers of cultural norms and traditions. In other words, a future world will either resemble a cookie-cutter American suburb or it will be a post-cultural space free of dominant norms.

This dichotomy raises several questions. First is a shared assumption that, broadly speaking, "tradition" and by implication norms and beliefs shared at a community level (the intangibles of heritage) are impediments to a future global world. Moreover, these perspectives tend to assume that global and local values, opinions, and norms

---

We begin this chapter by discussing traditional Chinese understandings of the relationship between nature and culture and how this relates to heritage preservation and tourism. After this, we discuss an ongoing national campaign aimed at increasing "civility," used in a broad sense to include civic consciousness, public behavior, and personal responsibility, and how this campaign intersects with environmental concerns, heritage projects, and the rapidly expanding domestic tourism industry. We conclude by noting key challenges that still remain.

R.J. Shepherd and L. Yu, *Heritage Management, Tourism, and Governance in China:*
Managing the Past to Serve the Present, SpringerBriefs in Archaeology 2,
DOI 10.1007/978-1-4614-5918-7_4, © Springer Science+Business Media, LLC 2013

are distinct and homogeneous (Weller 2006: 9). Anti-globalization advocates seek in vain for societies whose values and norms remain distinct (while they also campaign for transnational prescriptions such as human rights). Globalization advocates unreflectively embrace a Hegelian-Marxist view of history, as if some sort of cosmological law is at work.

The environmental and world heritage movements are excellent examples of this process. Much like the term "globalization," the environment is assumed by some people to be so self-evidently universal that any discussion of what precisely this term encompasses is deemed unnecessary. Instead, most debates about the environment are about protecting this from harm (preservation) or on ways of utilizing it for the greater good without permanent damage (conservation). Even more confusing is the concept of "nature," which is often conflated with "the environment." Proponents of protecting nature and/or the environment usually begin with three key assumptions: that nature and the environment are synonymous, that these are universal categories, and that they are separate from human-shaped space. Thus, "natural world heritage" from this perspective is by definition a natural space unsullied by human intervention. It follows that the value of nature preserves and parks lies in the extent to which they are free of permanent human presence,because nature without humanity is taken as intrinsically more authentically natural. This is a relatively recent concept in European thought, a product of the Enlightenment separation of subject and object as well as the scientific revolution's transformation of nature into a space not to be feared but a set of materials to be used (Weller 2006: 47). Indeed, until the late seventeenth century, nature, whether in the form of wilderness, forests, or mountains, had been a foreboding place for European and settler societies. It was not until the eighteenth century that these areas became objects of aesthetic contemplation. It took the Industrial Revolution to transform wild places from being untamed and dangerous to being untamed and therefore the site of the sublime. For an emerging class of wealthy elites in the eighteenth century, a reflection on nature could, it was believed, enable one to grapple with infinity. Nature also came to serve as a substitute for God at precisely the time that Enlightenment thought challenged religious faith.

The sacralization of nature remains a foundational aspect of environmentalism. Much like transnational human rights and development advocacy campaigns, the contemporary environmental movement takes as self-evident the claim that all humans belong to a world community whose values transcend cultural norms and practices. This is despite the fact that what Arun Agrawal (2005) has termed "environmentality" is a product of a specific cultural tradition and hence is far from universal. In Chinese, the most common translation of "nature" is *zi ran*, which connotes spontaneity and self-evident reality as part of the five elements of fire, water, earth, wood, and metal (Li and Sofield 2009: 159). This Chinese sense of nature does not infer a cosmological force or being that is the author of reality or an essential (and superior) quality (Weller 2006: 21). Thus, to say in Chinese that a product is "all natural" or that an event was an "act of nature" is much more difficult, simply because humans from a Chinese linguistic perspective are part of nature.

The Enlightenment separation of nature and culture has never been a part of Chinese classical thought. Instead, Confucianism stressed harmony between humans (and earth) and heaven (nature), with the world serving as a resource to be used for the improvement of civilized peoples. Daoism's ecocentric perspective situated humans within nature, while the biocentrism of Buddhism stressed the value of all life forms (Shapiro 2001: 213). If civilization (*wenming*) was identifiable by its possession of culture, the periphery was not different because it was closer to nature but because it lacked civility. Thus, although Daoism and Buddhism in China are identified with distinct sacred mountains, these have historically been destinations, not refuges from civilization (Wan and Xue 2008: 574). In other words, the space of nature, whether from a Confucian, Daoist, or Buddhist perspective, was not considered the antithesis of civilization. Instead, humans existed within a web of mutual dependency with each other and the world itself that spanned time and space. This anthropocosmic perspective links people with past and present in an (ideally) harmonious mutual dependence premised on a desire to tame and control not nature but *qi*, the energy force that emanates everywhere, as a means of both personal improvement and social order (Weller 2006: 23–29). Nature and the natural world in this sense are characterized by the pervasiveness of *qi*, the lack of any division between humans and the physical world, and an obligation for humans to utilize the physical world to benefit themselves and others.

From this traditional Chinese perspective, the spatial segregation of either culture or nature, in the form of gated heritage sites, nature preserves, or national parks, is premised on a fundamentally non-Chinese assumption (and one which clearly is not universal), namely, that heritage of all types is best maintained by being separated from existing social realities. The displacement of people in the name of heritage preservation, whether in China or elsewhere, is thus not a matter of logic but follows from specific cultural assumptions that originated in specific European societies at a specific time period. Indeed, any example of cultural heritage, be this a tangible object, building or site, or an intangible practice such as a song, poem, or other performance, is situated within an "eco-site" that gives it coherence (McLaren 2011: 431). This also illustrates the underlying paradox of preservation: led by UNESCO, the world heritage movement seeks to preserve cultural diversity during an era of globalization which is presumed to carry the eminent threat of cultural sameness, yet in doing so, this preservationist ideology mandates a specific spatial form of preservation that erases cultural differences and paradoxically evokes and promotes this sameness.

In summary, Chinese philosophical views of the relationship between humans and the world, the real and the fake, and nature and culture are at odds with both contemporary anthropocentric utilitarianism and the deep ecology of radical environmentalism. Nevertheless, contemporary Chinese society has been undergoing a modernization experiment for more than a century. During much of this period, Qing reformers, nationalists, and communists have all embraced policies and programs that have aimed at subjugating nature, culminating in the attacks on "old culture" in the 1960s and the mass resettlement of millions of urbanites in rural areas. These forced resettlement campaigns, first of suspected rightists purged in 1957 and later of youth sent down to the countryside during the Cultural Revolution, were in part aimed at opening up "nature" in remote areas such as Xinjiang, Qinghai, Inner Mongolia, and Manchuria (Weller 2006).

Under Mao, nature became an enemy to progress that had to be conquered. This position in itself was not that unusual during the era of high modernism that stretched roughly from the First World War until the collapse of the Soviet Union (Scott 1999). This period was characterized by a widespread faith in the transformative power of objective science, state planning, and the efficacy of economies of scale that transcended political and cultural division, underwritten by a dominant faith that life could be made both qualitatively and quantitatively better through state-directed planned interventions. The early decades of the Soviet Union, mega projects in the United States such as the Tennessee Valley Authority and Hoover Dam, and numerous development projects in postcolonial Africa and Asia sought to at least tame, if not conquer, nature. What made Mao's approach unusual (and in hindsight catastrophic) was the utopian element he added. His dictum that will-power trumps the laws of physics and biology, combined with the suppression of authentic scientific inquiry and all aspects of public debate, resulted in environmental disasters and a population explosion from which Chinese society has not recovered (Shapiro 2001: 8). Mao was thus unique because he rejected both traditional norms and scientific laws, effectively ending the *ti-yong* (essence versus use) debate that had dominated Chinese politics since the late Qing Dynasty. The question no longer was how to reconcile foreign technologies with an underlying essence of Chinese culture. Instead, the future would arrive through a state-directed attack on the natural world, constant personal sacrifice and self-cultivation, and the folk wisdom of the masses, most of whom were peasants.

This strange mix of Enlightenment authoritarianism, Neo-Confucianism, and peasant Romanticism is further complicated by Buddhism. For example, Buddhism's emphasis on the transience of reality raises practical questions about the underlying utility of preservation (an idealized material permanence). This does not mean that monastic communities cannot possess wealth, if its purpose is to support devotion (Kieschnick 2003: 6). In fact, after state attacks on Buddhism in 845 CE, the accumulation of material objects and wealth by monasteries and temples was never widely condemned in China until the nationalist and communist political movements in the early twentieth century. Strict preservation of material objects, however, has not been a priority of monastic authorities, as illustrated by the shared Buddhist and Confucian practice of temple renewal. This periodic renovation of monasteries and temples demonstrates how Chinese philosophy and religious practice do not emphasize material preservation or material authenticity (Zhang et al. 2007: 78).

Strict cultural preservation, then, has no philosophical, religious, or cultural basis in Chinese history. As already noted, Mao's attacks on China's material past were unique not in intention but only in the extent of the damage his policies caused. State-directed projects to harness the natural world such as dams, irrigation schemes, and the opening of distant lands date back to the earliest dynasties (Shapiro 2001: 195–196). In fact, Mao's utopian visions for transforming Chinese society illustrate the extent to which he was not a Marxist. It was Marx, after all, who transformed Hegel's universal historical narrative into a meta-narrative of class struggle by emphasizing the relationship between a society's material base and its relative social development. According to Marx, the material conditions of a given time and place dictated a society's stage of development, not vice versa. Thus, from a Marxist perspective, an overwhelmingly agrarian Chinese society could never achieve communism until it first achieved capitalism. Mao ignored this fundamental Marxist principle, insisting that the collective will of the Chinese people would enable then to transcend historical stages of development. The net result of the Great Leap Forward (1958–1961) and Cultural Revolution (1966–1976) was economic disruption, mass famine, widespread violence, and in the case of the latter, incipient civil war until army intervention.

Following Mao's death in 1976, Deng Xiaoping shifted the state and party focus away from the politicization of all aspects of life in favor of pragmatism aimed at material prosperity under the guidance of the CCP. However, while advocating the efficacy of markets to raise living standards, neither Deng nor his successors have accepted the idea that market forces should be allowed to shape social and moral behavior. The first "spiritual civilization campaign" (*jingshen wenhua yundong*) was launched by Deng in 1982. Unlike Maoist political campaigns, this was not a campaign based on class struggle. Indeed, the language of class was noticeably absent. Instead, this stressed public morality, patriotism, culture, and self-discipline. Serving as a unifying theme for all of these points was the term "civilization" itself. In 1997 the State Council established the Central Commission for Building Spiritual Civilization (*zhongyang jingshen weming jianshe zhidao weiyuanwei*), tasked with promoting a set of idealized social norms as models of behavior for peasants and workers under the rubric of civilization. This was followed by a 2004 campaign by President Hu Jintao promoting a harmonious society that balances material growth, political stability, a proper spiritual basis, and environmental awareness (Dynon 2008).

At the heart of these state campaigns is the term *wenming*, which translates as "civilized" or "civilization" but in contemporary China connotes "civility." This term is displayed prominently in the public sphere in China. Calls for people to act civilized and be civilized are found on billboards, in television commercials, and even in school textbooks (Fig. 4.1).

While a relatively recent phenomena, this *wenming* campaign has its roots in a century-old debate about how to be simultaneously modern and Chinese. *Wenming* is not actually a Chinese word but a cultural borrowing from Meiji Japan (Friedman 2004) and entered the Chinese language at approximately the same time period (the decade of the 1880s) as *minzu*, variously translated as "ethnicity," "race," and "clan" (Erbaugh 2008: 639). Like its Japanese equivalent *bunmei*, *wenming* has two distinct connotations, one mental and spiritual and the other material (Anagnost 1997: 82). For the former, *wenming* describes an unbroken historical tradition of 5000 years, which makes China unique in the world. As noted in Chap. 3, this claim of a homogeneous history is evident not just in popular Han Chinese culture but also in heritage spaces such as the National Museum of China in Beijing, where it is presented as an objective truth and evidence of the territorial, cultural, and ethnic unity of the peoples of China.

However, *wenming* also carries a very different meaning, describing the dynamics of an emerging civil, modern society. This is a society that is civilized because it is peopled by productive, efficient, responsible, and disciplined citizens who are

Fig. 4.1 "Establishing civility requires everyone's participation": banner along a pedestrian walkway in suburban Beijing, 2011

capable of checking their own personal behavior for the greater good (Friedman 2004). "Civilized" from this perspective is radically different than what is imagined by advocates of a Lockean "civil society." Rather than a society filled with actors whose interests clash in a public sphere governed by agreed-upon rules of behavior, citizens possessing the proper *wenming* practice sanctioned hygiene, manners, family habits, and thinking, without the need of supervision (Nyiri 2006 [b]: 88). It is a modern society much more akin to Singapore than to the United States or for that matter Taiwan.

This ideal civil society is guided by the moral attributes of *suzhi* (quality) and *wenhua* (culture). Critics have dismissed government programs focused on improving people's *suzhi* as an attempt to exploit peasants in new ways (Yan 2003), impose new family practices (Aragnost 1997 [b]), or construct neoliberal subjects (Kipnis 2007: 385). However, from the state and party perspective, *suzhi* reflects a person's physical, mental, and moral development (Kipnis 2006; Jacka 2009). To possess the right sort of *suzhi* is to be both modern and Chinese or to be modern in a suitably Chinese way. This idea has deep historical roots in Chinese history and philosophy, reflecting a Confucian emphasis on continual self-reflection and improvement as a means of striving toward an ideal state of complete humaneness (*ren*). It also reflects the post-1949 Communist Party emphasis on the complete development of individuals (economic, physical, psychological, and moral) in the making of a new China (Murphy 2004).

This relentless emphasis on personal quality is not simply state propaganda. Increasing numbers of urban middle- and upper-class elites have embraced this as well.

No longer Maoist "enemies of the people," these beneficiaries of economic and social reforms have become key stakeholders in contemporary Chinese society. This new elite does not necessarily contest either the state or the party because it is part of both the state and party moral project of development (Jacka 2009: 526). This is also the case in regard to heritage. From a CCP development perspective, there is no contradiction between preserving heritage sites and promoting mass tourism at these sites. This is because tourism will presumably boost material development in areas that lack resources other than culture. But it will also boost spiritual development by bringing higher quality urban residents into contact with the rural inhabitants of heritage sites. By serving as models of proper civil behavior, this new class of consumer elites will guide rural residents toward a modern sensibility (Shepherd 2012).

This discourse of population quality neatly intersects with a state ethnic classification project that began shortly after the establishment of the People's Republic in 1949. In 1954 teams of social scientists were dispatched across the country to enumerate all citizens of the new republic. The primary criteria used to classify people were language, mode of production, customs, and the Stalinist concept of "common psychological makeup." These criteria were drawn from Marx's historical materialist approach to history, which theorizes that all societies pass through universal stages of primitive communism, slavery, feudalism, capitalism, and finally socialism. The purpose of this ethnic project was to determine the demographic makeup of the PRC and the relative development status of various peoples. The net result was a population of 55 official ethnic minorities, comprising approximately 9% of the population, and the Han majority. While each minority group was deemed to possess customs (*minsu*) such as music, dress styles, and particular foods, "culture" (*wenhua*) was the domain of the center. Indeed, *wenhua* literally means a transformation toward a qualitatively and more advanced level of learning and knowledge. Using this logic, not all ethnic groups can possess culture, since to do so would mean that all ethnic groups are equally advanced.

Instead, Marxist theory suggested that customs and traditions (what we now call intangible heritage) must inevitably disappear as a particular society advances through the universal stages of development. Thus, from the state and party view in the 1950s, an ethnic classification project would both help the state see all of its subjects (Mullaney 2010) and document differences that would soon be erased. This project also fits with the ethno-nationalist politics of Sun Yat-sen, who as we have seen argued that Han people had a duty to first overthrow the foreign regime of the Qing before subsuming their own ethnic identity into a modern Chinese identity. However, in the PRC, the classification of less-developed official minorities served to reinforce the view that not only are Han more advanced and therefore have a duty to assist the development of non-Han but that minority peoples can only become modern through in effect, becoming Han (Blum 2000: 72–75). This is not a view that has been imposed by the Communist Party. Instead, it is rooted in deep historical and popular assumptions about the location of culture in the dominant center (Tuohy 1991). The more than century-long modernization project undertaken by, in turn, late Qing reformers, Republican-era officials and warlords, Maoists, and most recently CCP pragmatists has occurred within these long-held assumptions of a particular group's perceived cultural distance from the center (Oakes 1997: 46).

This equating of distance, both in terms of space and shared social practices, with one's relative civility has been reinforced by *suzhi* discourse. However, no longer are people forever hindered by their ethnic status in advancing; through a personal transformation individuals can, at least in theory, become "higher-quality" citizens. They can do so through a rejection of quantity (in family size) and a dedication to education. Education is, from this perspective, not simply a matter of formal training and testing (Murphy 2004). It is also, as noted above, a personal process of constant self-reflection, not on how to be a good Confucian subject, but on how to be a proper modern citizen. And heritage serves a crucial role in this process, instructing visitors not simply about the past but more importantly the present. Just as migrant workers are supposed to bring a measure of *suzhi* and *wenming* back to their rural communities from more advanced and modern urban areas, cosmopolitan urbanites are supposed to bring the same with them when they tour heritage destinations. In this way, tourism is tasked with raising the levels of civility of both tourists and local residents of toured sites (Nyiri 2009: 154).

In recent years, the central government has begun to promote the concept of "ecological civilization" (*shengtai wenming*) that, along with "scientific development," will bring sustainable modernization (McLaren 2011: 429). This shift in focus aims to foster a heritage and ecological discourse that supports development objectives aimed at both material and what the Communist Party has called "spiritual" (*jingshen*) development. Of course, one of the central paradoxes in this approach is the fact that this same political party in the not so distant past sought to destroy all aspects of heritage in pursuit of these same development goals. Consequently, thousands of heritage sites have been renovated, restored, or in many cases, completely recreated in the last two decades. From a Euro-American perspective, a clear problem exists: to what extent can relatively new heritage sites be attractive destinations for tourists?

In societies in which the authenticity of material culture is judged by its ontological significance and antiquity, any rebuilt, renovated, or reconstructed sites and copied objects are intrinsically suspect, never quite real, and forever verging on the fake. But the relationship between copies and originals in China has traditionally been quite different than post-Enlightenment modernist notions. A copy, be this of nature or of built space, traditionally was not viewed as a lesser version of an original and thus a cheapening of some sort of original aura. Rather, a copy gave the possessor a degree of power over the original (Elliot and Shambaugh 2005: 22). For example, the twelve-century Song emperor Huizong had an elaborate hunting park built that depicted the world in miniature, a practice the eighteenth century Qing Emperors Qianlong and Kangxi copied when they commissioned an elaborate mountain resort filled with replicas of famous Buddhist temples, important sites in China, and even a Great Wall in miniature, near the present-day city of Chengde in Hebei province. These sites were not regarded as "mere" copies (and therefore of less intrinsic value); they instead reflected the power of the ruler and his ability to harness both nature and built space. This is similar to Chinese and

Fig. 4.2 The refurbished Sumtseling (Songzanlin) Monastery (built 1659), the largest Tibetan Buddhist monastery in Yunnan, located in Zhongdian County (*Tibetan Gyalthung*). The complex was shelled by People's Liberation Army Forces in 1959 and attacked by Red Guards during the Cultural Revolution

Japanese approaches to landscape gardening, which aims to replicate nature in miniature. Quite predictably, the concept of authenticity, which is central to heritage discussions, does not translate well into Chinese. Whereas the "authentic" is generally rendered as "the real" or "the original" in English (in contrast to a fake or a copy), the Chinese term *zhenshixing* ("true facts essence") connotes verifiability. In other words, the issue is not so much whether a copy is a copy; it is whether it is a good copy, one that is faithful to what it mirrors.

This partly explains the sheer quantity of heritage sites in China in the wake of the Cultural Revolution. As noted in Chap. 3, while historically important sites such as the Forbidden City were protected by the military, the vast majority of public heritage sites were looted, damaged, and desecrated by Red Guard factions, especially in 1966. The domestic tourism boom that began in the 1990s has stimulated an intensive campaign of heritage refurbishment, renovation, and in some cases wholesale reconstruction.

For example, temple construction, be this Buddhist or Daoist, often is aimed at tourism and economic development more than supporting religious intentions. In Zhongdian, Yunnan province, a frontier town on the Chinese and Tibetan border that has been promoted by provincial and county authorities as the "real" Shangri-La, the local government has invested significant resources to reconstruct Songze Monastery, which had been largely destroyed by Red Guards (Fig. 4.2). Similarly, a

Fig. 4.3 The newly built Wenshu (Manjusri) Temple, Mount Wutai, Shanxi, a world heritage site

desire to attract Hong Kong tourists has led local authorities in Jinhua Township in Zhejiang province to finance the construction of a temple dedicated to the Daoist God Wong Tai Sin, who legends say lived in the area in the fourth century CE (Chan 2005: 66). Local attempts to capture this tourist market led to the eventual construction of five different such temples. But the authenticity of these temples cannot be evaluated based on their historical claims or physical structures. Instead, the popularity of these sites with Hong Kong tourists who visit for both pleasure and faith reasons has authenticated them for local residents. Competing ontological claims of authenticity among these different temples were resolved by fiat by local authorities in 1995 when they declared that Wong had been born, lived, and become a saint in different places, thus making all of these (new) temples "authentic" (ibid, 70–72).

In addition, the verifiability of a cultural site has traditionally been linked to its geographic location and not to buildings or artifacts. For example, local monastic authorities recently completed the construction of a new temple dedicated to Wenshu (Manjusri, the Buddha of Wisdom) inside the core heritage zone of Mount Wutai National Park, which is also a UNESCO world heritage site and therefore in theory not subject to new construction (Shepherd 2012) (Fig. 4.3). In Gansu's Gannan Tibetan Autonomous Prefecture, ongoing renovations have repaired most of the damage done during the Cultural Revolution, including the completely new Gong

Tang pagoda. In Gannan's capital, Hezuo, Milarapa Temple was built in the late seventeenth century, completely destroyed during the Cultural Revolution, and reconstructed between 1988 and 1992. Given that the overwhelming majority of visitors to these sites are Tibetans and Han Chinese, the ontological question of their authenticity is largely irrelevant. In fact, one could argue that the absence of a privileging of the ontological basis of material culture is productive, both for tourism and religion.

Other challenges, however, remain. Central among these is the sheer size of the tourism industry in China, which we discuss in Chap. 5. How to cope with more than one billion tourist trips each year? How to balance accessibility with preservation and conservation worries? Connected to this is how tourism functions in China. What makes a trip satisfying? As noted above, Chinese culture has no historic or philosophical tradition of privileging nature over culture or the relative purity of nature. Scenic spots are attractive not because they are "natural" but because they are well developed, attract visitors, credentialed, spatially mapped, and standardized (Nyiri 2006: 49–54). Nature is not regarded as sacred nor is there any location of authenticity in a supposedly natural realm of purity. Instead, a good trip is satisfying because it is social, not solitary. Performance (of cultural practices and of nature itself) is both expected and valued; there is no valorization of everyday life as intrinsically more authentic and hence desirable.

This leads to further challenges in, for example, the promotion of environmental tourism. In surveys of visitors to Lake Bita and Mount Taibai in Shanxi province, Wan and Xue (2008) found that the majority of Chinese tourists did not identify with environmentalist values. Far from seeing tourism in natural areas as an escape from civilization or as a chance to physically challenge themselves, these respondents viewed such experiences as no different than any other tourist destination. Ecotourism norms such as sustainability and escape carried little resonance with these visitors. Nationally, tourism to nature sites remains dominated by mass tourism. This example points to an underlying paradox in the promotion of environmental tourism in China: the dominant indigenous views toward nature (a mix of Confucian, Daoist, Buddhist, and Maoist norms and assumptions) do not privilege nature or the environment and do not recognize these as distinct spaces that must be treated as sacred. Instead, nature is expected to be just as social, crowded, and lively as civilization. Yet to become environmentally conscious requires people to view nature in a very different way, as a sacred space distinct from civilization that is visited for aesthetic and contemplative reasons. In other words, domestic tourists need to adopt transnational norms about the environment and thus become westernized – although state authorities insist that China is following a development path that is based on its own unique characteristics.

At least to this point in the reform process, mass tourism in China has not been driven by a reaction against modernization. In other words, there is no widespread desire to "go back to nature." Instead, "nature" is supposed to be developed to meet the expectations of visitors. Paradoxically, this is also increasingly the case for built heritage space, particularly in urban areas. This is a challenge we turn to in our next chapter.

Bibliography

Agrawal, Arun. 2005. *Environmentality: Technologies of Government and the Making of Subjects*. Durham: Duke University, Press.

Anagnost, Ann. 1997. *National past-times: Narrative, representation, and power in China*. Durham: Duke University Press.

Anagnost, Ann. 2004. The corporeal politics of quality (*Suzhi*). *Public Culture* 16(2): 189–208. Spring.

Blum, Deborah. 2000. *Portrait of "Primitives": The making of human kinds in the Chinese nation*. Landam: Rowman & Littlefield.

Chan, Selina Ching. 2005. Temple building and heritage in China. *Ethnology* 44(1): 65–79.

Dynon, Nicholas. 2008. Four civilizations: The evolution of post-Mao Chinese socialist ideology. *The China Journal* 60: 83–109.

Elliot, Jeannette, with David Shambaugh. 2005. *The odyssey of China's imperial art treasures*. Seattle: University of Washington.

Erbaugh, Mary. 2008. China expands its courtesy: Saying "Hello" to strangers. *Journal of Asian Studies* 67(2): 621–652.

Friedman, Sara. 2004. Embodying civility: Civilizing processes and symbolic citizenship in southeast China. *Journal of Asian Studies* 63(3): 687–718.

Hairong, Yan. 2003. Neoliberal governmentality and neohumanism: Organizing suzhi/value flow through labor recruitment networks. *Cultural Anthropology* 18(4): 493–523.

Jacka, Tamara. 2009. Cultivating citizens: Quality (*suzhi*) discourse in the PRC. *Positions* 17(3): 523–535.

Kieschnick, John. 2003. *The impact of Buddhism on Chinese material culture*. Princeton: Princeton University Press.

Kipnis, Andrew. 2007. Neoliberalism reified: Suzhi discourse and tropes of neoliberalism in the PRC. *The Journal of the Royal Anthropological Institute* 13: 383–400.

Kipnis, Andrew. 2006. Suzhi: A keyword approach. *China Quarterly*, pp. 295–313.

Li Fung Mei, and Trevor Sofield. 2009. Huangshan (Yellow Mountain), China: The meaning of harmonious relationships. In *Tourism in China: Destinations, cultures, and communities*, ed. Chris Ryan and Gu Huimin, 157–167. London: Routledge.

McLaren, Anne. 2011. Environment and cultural heritage in China: Introduction. *Asian Studies Review* 35: 429–437.

Mullaney, Thomas. 2010. Seeing for the state: The role of social scientists in China's ethnic classification project. *Asian Ethnicity* 11(3): 325–342.

Murphy, Rachel. 2004. Turning peasants into modern Chinese citizens: "Population Quality" discourse, demographic transition, and primary education. *China Quarterly* 177: 1–20.

Nyiri, Pal. 2006. *Scenic spots: Chinese tourism, the state, and cultural authority*. Seattle: University of Washington.

Nyiri, Pal. 2009. Between encouragement and control: Tourism, modernity and discipline in China. In *Asia on tour: Exploring the rise of Asian tourism*, ed. T. Winter, P. Teo, and T.C. Chang, 153–169. London: Routledge.

Oakes, Timothy. 1997. Ethnic tourism in rural Guizhou: Sense of place and the commerce of authenticity. In *Tourism, ethnicity, and the state in Asian and Pacific societies*, ed. Michel Picard and Robert Wood, 35–70. Honolulu: University of Hawai'i Press.

Scott, James. 1999. *Seeing like a state: How certain schemes to improve the human condition have failed*. Chicago: University of Chicago Press.

Shapiro, Judith. 2001. *Mao's war against nature: Politics and the environment in revolutionary China*. Cambridge/New York: Cambridge University Press.

Shepherd, Robert. 2012. *Faith in heritage: Displacement, development, and religious tourism in contemporary China*. Walnut Grove: Left Coast Press.

Tuohy, Sue. 1991. Cultural metaphors and reasoning. *Asian Folklore Studies* 50: 189–220.

Weller, Robert. 2006. *Discovering nature: Globalization and environmental culture in China and Taiwan*. Cambridge, UK: Cambridge University Press.

Ye, Wan, and Xue Yiming. 2008. The differences in ecotourism between China and the West. *Current Issues in Tourism* 11(6): 567–586.

Zhang Mu, Huang Li, Wang Jianhong, Liu Ji, Jie Yangeng, and Lai Xiting. 2007. Religious tourism and cultural pilgrimage: A Chinese perspective. In *Religious tourism and pilgrimage management: An alternative perspective*, ed. R. Raj and N.D. Morpeth, 98–112. Cambridge, MA: CABI.

Chapter 5
Economics of Heritage Management

A key issue in the study of heritage tourism is reconciling the interests of heritage conservation and tourism promotion or an emphasis on the protection of heritage sites versus the utilization of these same sites for economic development purposes. How to preserve the past while fostering the consumption of this? More to the point, how to preserve the multiplicity of the past when heritage becomes a development resource?

As we have argued, heritage is a product of a selective process. Just as "the past" in either a general or holistic sense is not the target of preservation, neither is heritage. Instead, preservation is a dynamic process that selects, shapes, and reconstructs the past as much as it preserves this. This leads to a more vexing question, based on an often-cited fact, that tourism is now the world's largest industry: "how to reconstruct the past in the present through interpretation via global tourism in order to satisfy the needs of tourist consumption?" (Li 2003: 249). Framed in the context of globalization, heritage tourism appears to be both a potential means of protecting unique cultural resources from the assumed monocultural world of globalization and a potential means to creating this monocultural world. In other words, does heritage tourism enable the protection of uniqueness or facilitate sameness, transforming material cultural into a uniform space, much like transnational transportation, where

---

This chapter explores the economic foundations of heritage projects in China. It explains how "heritage" is classified and discusses the implications for placing national and world heritage sites under the domain of the Ministry of Construction, particularly in regard to tourism promotion. The decentralization of the management of heritage sites to local government units has also sharply impacted sites, as most of China's heritage sites are locally funded and consequently are viewed as revenue sources. The outsourcing of services and in some cases overall management of heritage sites raise serious questions about the balance between cultural preservation and nature conservation on the one hand and the commercialization of sites for profit on the other. Even in cases of serious potential harm to the integrity of a site, protection may not follow. This illustrates the declining influence of the State Administration of Cultural Heritage (SACH) and raises questions about whether the public good is always served by decentralization in all areas of governance.

R.J. Shepherd and L. Yu, *Heritage Management, Tourism, and Governance in China:*   47
Managing the Past to Serve the Present, SpringerBriefs in Archaeology 2,
DOI 10.1007/978-1-4614-5918-7_5, © Springer Science+Business Media, LLC 2013

the same planes, trains, and airport and highway designs, even the same signage, are found throughout the world?

This enduring tension between heritage preservationists and tourism advocates requires context, often the missing ingredient in theoretical debates about the effects of globalization. In the case of heritage and tourism in China, the intended audience is clearly not global, since fewer than 10% of the country's annual tourists are foreign. According to the China National Tourism Organization (CNTO), an average of 1.6 billion domestic tourist trips are made by PRC citizens each year, whereas foreign arrivals average 130 million (CNTO 2009). And, of this foreign sector, more than 80% are ethnic Chinese residents of Hong Kong, Taiwan, and Macau. In other words, just over 1% (approximately 22 million) of the more than 1.7 billion annual tourist trips in China are undertaken by people who are not ethnically Han Chinese. Tourism in China is thus largely a Chinese phenomenon and a return to a long tradition of travel and pilgrimage that was disrupted between 1911 and 1976 by revolution, war, and ideological extremism (Sofield and Li 1998: 363). However, what is different in the current situation is the democratization of travel in China. No longer is travel restricted to cultural and political elites. Instead, tourism in China gives truth to the phrase "mass travel," which has shifted the cultural debate. Rather than a process of promoting the self to others, tourism is about promoting the self to oneself.

The Administrative Structure

As noted in Chap. 3, the first attempt to categorize cultural heritage after 1949 was the designation of 180 Nationally Protected Sites of Significant Cultural Relics in March 1961 (Xie 2002; State Administration of Cultural Heritage 2012). These significant cultural relics were first identified and classified as nonremovable objects, buildings, and sites with historic, artistic, or scientific value at local administrative levels and then verified by the State Council, China's ultimate authorities. Since this first designation, the State Council has issued five additional decrees listing significant cultural relics in China. The last, in 2006, brought this list of national heritage sites to 1,080 (State Administration of Cultural Heritage 2006).

To meet the increasing demand for tourism planning and development in the early 1980s, the Ministry of Construction (now renamed the Ministry of Housing and Urban–rural Development) was vested by the State Council to take on two key responsibilities that deal with cultural heritage. The first was to review and approve the designation of National Historical and Cultural Cities and supervise their preservation and protection; the second was to approve plans for National Scenic Areas and manage land use within these (Ministry of Housing and Urban–rural Development 2012). In 1982, the Ministry of Construction released its first list of 24 National Historical and Cultural Cities and 44 National Scenic Areas. By the end of 2009, 120 cities had been classified as protected urban sites, and 208 national scenic spots had been identified (Ministry of Housing and Urban–rural Development 2010). In addition, by 2000, China had approximately 1,000 nature reserves (Weller 2006: 77).

Fig. 5.1 Yungang Grottoes (fifth century CE), Datong, Shanxi province, a 5A national scenic site

In addition to national scenic areas, each province has also identified and recognized a second tier of scenic sites that are supervised by provincial-level Bureaus of
Construction, as have municipalities and counties. A five-tier ranking system is used
to classify the quality of all scenic areas, ranging from 5A (AAAAA) to 1A (A) des-
ignations, similar to the five-star ranking system for hotel operations in China. The
5A scenic areas are typically the iconic natural and cultural attractions in different
parts of the country. The 5A scenic sites with cultural and historical significance are
also cross-listed as nationally protected cultural heritage sites. An applicant for 5A
recognition is evaluated on 12 criteria, including tourism resources, conservation,
infrastructure, management operation, safety, and the level of visitor interest and
satisfaction. The 4A scenic areas are mostly well-known attractions at the national
and provincial levels. The lower-ranking scenic areas (3A–1A) are normally found
at the city and county levels. This ranking program is overseen by the China National
Tourism Administration (CNTA), while site assessments and recommendations
are made by the National Tourism Scenic Area Quality Assessment Commission
(Fig. 5.1).

As noted in Chap. 3, heritage preservation has been explicitly defined in political
terms by the national government as well as by the Communist Party. For example, the
State Administration of Cultural Heritage (SACH) has stated that the purpose of cultural heritage is to "strengthen national unity and promote sustainable development of

the national culture" (Agnew and Demas 2004: 59). Local authorities, on the other hand, tend to view cultural heritage in terms of its economic and thus development potential (Shen and Chen 2010: 72). Development and culture, far from being viewed as antithetical, are seen as complements by many bureaucrats: existing cultural resources can drive economic development, which will in turn produce more cultured subjects (Nyiri 2006: 80). This is important because beginning in 1998, state authorities shifted control of tourism and heritage management to provinces, municipalities, and counties as part of a broader administrative decentralization effort. As more and more locales compete to capture part of the domestic tourism market as a revenue source, they seek a comparative advantage by promoting (and in some cases reconstructing or even creating) their own unique heritage sites.

The net result is a heritage field that is largely unregulated. As of 2,000, SACH listed approximately 300,000 recognized heritage sites; 7,000 provincial, regional, and municipal protected sites; and 1,268 national sites (Zhang 2004: 91). But a decade later, it estimated China had more than 400,000 heritage sites, of which 2,351 were officially recognized national sites, approximately 9,300 were recognized at the provincial level, and 58,000 were recognized by either municipal or county authorities. In other words, the State Administration of Cultural Heritage itself estimates that less than 20% of the country's potential heritage sites receive any sort of state protection (Shen and Chen 2010: 72).

Management of Cultural Heritage

A crucial issue for heritage preservation is funding. Who should pay for preservation and conservation, and how should these programs be funded? Realizing the economic value of cultural heritage for tourism development, government agencies, planning professionals, and tourism companies have experimented with different models of cultural heritage management operations since the late 1990s. The decentralization of government that began at that time provided more authority in decision making to local officials but also required them to generate their own revenue sources. Moreover, officials are evaluated mainly by their success in promoting economic development. This leads them to emphasize short-term results (Li et al. 2008).

At present, management of cultural heritage for tourism in China is characterized by three distinct models: government control, joint ventures between local governments and private management companies, and private management contracting. Government management is still the prevalent management practice in China. In this case, the provincial, municipal, or county government appoints a commission to manage a cultural heritage site. Its operating budget comes from the responsible government authority, and its profits go back to the government treasury. The Zhoukoudian Peking Man site is an example of cultural heritage under government management but has been criticized for a lack of planning and low attendance levels (Wang 2002). An example of the second model is Shao Lin Temple, situated in the core zone of a UNESCO world heritage site and also a 5A scenic site. Management in this case is a joint venture between China Travel Service Hong Kong and the Dengfeng Municipal Government. A joint-venture company, CTS HK-Dengfeng Songshan Shao Lin Cultural Tourism Limited, was established in 2009 with a 51%/49% split. The management agreement granted control of all operations in the Song Shan Scenic Area to this entity (Liu 2012). The third model, while less common, is growing. In this case, the local government leases a cultural heritage site to a private firm for a set fee. In return, the private company is required to invest, develop, and manage the cultural heritage site. Bifengxia near Ya'an City in Sichuan province was one of the first such sites (Li 2002; Huang 2004). In 1998, the city of Ya'an signed a lease agreement with the Wan Guan Group, a Chinese private company, to develop and operate Bifengxia scenic area, setting up the Bifengxia model for natural and cultural heritage sites management for tourism development. The lease agreement stipulates that the state owns the assets of the scenic area, the local government holds administrative authority over the scenic area, and Wan Guan Group holds a 50-year lease to develop, protect, and operate the scenic area without interference by either the government or the state (Shen 2011; Xu 2005).

Chinese scholars in a range of disciplines have hotly debated structural reform of the management system for China's cultural and natural heritage resources. This debate can be summarized as a management transfer model versus a national park model (Yu et al. 2006). The proponents of privatizing management cite the financial success of publically traded tourism companies that manage heritage sites as a reason for the transfer of management rights from state control to private companies operating under a market-driven model based on the economic utilization of cultural heritage (Wei 2000; Wang 2002). They assert that this model frees local and provincial authorities from funding heritage sites at a time when the national government has sharply curtailed its contributions. This also creates a new revenue source while allowing the state to maintain its ownership of these sites. One of the most cited examples of this model is the Huangshan (Yellow Mountain) Tourism Development Company Ltd., one of the earliest public tourism companies managing cultural heritage. This company was listed on the Shanghai Stock Exchange in November 1996 after it was formed through a consolidation of site management, a cable car business, hotels, and tour operations at one of the country's most famous tourist destinations, Yellow Mountain in Anhui province. Under an agreement with local authorities, HTD took over complete control of Yellow Mountain National Park, including maintenance, sanitation, development, and finances. By 2,000, the company had completely paid back the ¥190 million debt accumulated under local government management in the past (Wang 2002). The company is now a highly diversified tourism company with an estimated capitalization of ¥7.2 billion ($1.1 billion). It also has been recognized for its management of cultural and natural heritage resources by the provincial and national governments as well as by the UNESCO Heritage Committee. Another example is Mount E'mei (E'meishan) in Sichuan province, a national park and world heritage site that is completely managed by the publicly listed E'meishan Tourism Development Company.

However, proponents of the national park model counter that cultural heritage belongs to all citizens and its preservation and management should be first and foremost for public welfare. They argue that the transfer of heritage site management to private companies contradicts this because these companies seek a profit as their main goal. Thus market-based management plans effectively transform public goods into private assets (Zhang and Zhen 2001). Furthermore, scholars arguing for a national park model contend that the separation of management and operation responsibilities inevitably leads to the commercial exploitation of cultural heritage assets and eventually the destruction of heritage resources (Xu 2003). As evidence, they cite cases where tourism facilities have been built at a heritage site without any environmental impact analysis. For example, Wulingyuan, a thickly forested region in Hunan famous for its extensive karst topography of more than 3,000 quartz sandstone pillars, was inscribed on the world heritage list in 1992. After management of the site was privatized, a network of cable cars was constructed in the area, linking some of these pillars, which can be as high as 800 m. One such cable car was built in Zhangjiajie National Park, located in the middle of Wulingyuan. Opened in 1999 at a cost of ¥120 million, the *Bailong Tianti* cable car was touted by park managers as the fastest outdoor sightseeing cable car in the world, with a carrying capacity of 18,000 visitors daily. However, this was shut down by the Ministry of Construction in 2002 and only resumed operations 1 year later because there had been no environmental assessment when it was built (Xu et al. 2006). Furthermore, rapid tourism construction in the area has led to water pollution problems as well as the cutting of protected forest areas (Peng 2001). This has resulted in Wulingyuan being put on notice by the UNESCO World Heritage Commission for overbuilding tourism facilities to accommodate increased tourist arrivals (Liang et al. 2009). This case also illustrates a key problem with completely privatized management of heritage sites: private contractors are obligated to their investors and shareholders, not the public at large. Consequently, conservation or preservation policies that are not profitable will not be popular under this arrangement.

The complexity of ownership, management, and law enforcement responsibilities has presented many challenges to cultural heritage management. These include a lack of coordination and at times a conflict of interest among different state agencies at the local, provincial, and national levels; an absence of real authority for planners and site managers to implement and enforce planning and development codes; and tensions and disagreements between government officials, private investors, and local communities (Jiang 2010) (Fig. 5.2).

First, identifying, assessing, and managing the objects and sites signifying cultural heritage fall under the domain of many government agencies (Wang 2002). Management authority at heritage sites is fragmented both vertically and horizontally. For example, in addition to the State Administration of Cultural Heritage and the Ministry of Housing and Urban–rural Development (formerly the Bureau of Construction), the Bureau of Religious Affairs, under the jurisdiction of the State Council, began identifying and listing important Buddhist monasteries and Daoist temples as heritage sites in 1983. Meanwhile, the Ministry of Culture is now experimenting with a new heritage category of 12 National Protected Cultural Ecology areas (*guojiaji wenhua shengtai baohuqu*), designed to preserve nonmaterial cultural heritage unique to specific regions of the country (Liu 2007). The designation and administration of monuments, memorials, and cemeteries commemorating war

Fig. 5.2 The Great Wall near Mutianyu, Beijing municipality. This section of the Wall was originally built during the sixth century CE

martyrs have been under the jurisdiction of the Ministry of Civil Affairs since 1986. Archeological sites are approved and jointly managed by the Ministry of Housing and Urban–rural Development and the State Administration of Cultural Heritage, but geological formations at these sites are managed by the Ministry of Geology. This complicated administrative structure presents great challenges, especially at sites that combine natural and cultural attributes and consequently must respond to multiple agencies.

Mount Wutai, a sacred Buddhist mountain area designated a national park in 1982 and inscribed as a world heritage site in 2009, illustrates this fragmented bureaucratic structure of competing interests. Overall management authority is shared by the Ministry of Housing and Urban–rural Development and the Construction Authority of Shanxi Province. But the park's forest reserves are overseen by the State Forestry Administration, temple sites by the State Administration of Cultural Heritage, religious practice at temples and monasteries by the State Administration for Religious Affairs, geological sites by the Ministry of Geology, fossils by the Ministry of Land and Resources, and tourism by the National Tourism Administration. Finally, 29 different international, national, and provincial conventions, laws, and decrees impact the site (Shepherd 2012). These range from the 1972 Convention on World Heritage and various State Council decrees on heritage protection to national laws regulating geological heritage (1995), forests (1998), fossils (2002), cultural relics (2003), religious practice (2004), and scenic areas (2006) (Fig. 5.3).

Fig. 5.3 Tayuan Temple (sixteenth century), Mount Wutai, Shanxi province

Far from being unique, the management complexities found at Mount Wutai are quite common. Table 5.1 lists the range of government agencies in Sichuan province that have direct regulatory responsibilities for tourism management issues at provincial cultural heritage sites.

This fragmented authority is accentuated at heritage sites such as Jiuzhaigou National Park that fall under the regulatory oversight of several different government agencies with widely different objectives leading to policies and regulations that are not always consistent. To address this lack of coordinated decision making, all major cultural heritage sites have Tourism Scenic Area Management Committees which (in theory) enjoy equal administrative stature with municipal or county governments. The Committee's operating budgets are funded by the local municipal or prefecture government, and profits go back to the government treasury. To ensure a close relationship between cultural heritage management and local governments, key positions of the Committees are held by top local officials. This solution, however, raises additional questions. Because government officials are evaluated primarily on their success in achieving demonstrable economic growth, and because a job promotion usually means a transfer to a new location, local officials have little incentive to consider the long-term impact of their planning and management decisions on a heritage site. In other words, loans taken to pay for heritage site development or the future sustainability of a management plan are left for others to navigate.

As already mentioned, the day-to-day operation of part or all of a cultural heritage site may be leased to one or more companies under a management contract. At the majority of Chinese heritage sites of whatever level services such as cable

Table 5.1 Regulatory agencies involved with cultural heritage sites in Sichuan province

Type of attraction	Number	Regulatory agency
World heritage sites	5	Construction Bureau
		Land Resource Bureau
		Forestry Bureau
		Water Resource Bureau
		Cultural Heritage Bureau
		Religious Affairs Office
		Env. Protection Agency
National A-level scenic sites (5A and 4A)	156 (21)	Construction Bureau
		Land Resource Bureau
		Forestry Bureau
		Water Resource Bureau
		Cultural Heritage Bureau
		Religious Affairs Office
		Env. Protection Bureau
National (provincial) level important scenic and historic interest area	15 (90)	Construction Bureau
		Env. Protection Bureau
National (provincial) level registry of historical and cultural cities and towns	7 (32)	Construction Bureau
		Cultural Heritage Bureau
National (provincial) level cultural relics	62 (360)	Construction
		Cultural Heritage Bureau
		Religious Affairs Office
Museums of various themes and exhibits	63	Cultural Heritage Bureau
		Various agencies
Patriotic educational sites	55	Internal Affair Bureau
		Various agencies

Source: Sichuan Travel and Tourism Administration 2012

cars, tourist buses, food and beverage services, and souvenir retailers are now mostly provided by individual companies and vendors rather than by site management. However, the companies that are awarded contracts for cable cars and tourist buses are often state-owned or have significant shares held by the local government, which blurs distinctions between public and private.

A large number of laws, regulations, and implementation guidelines have been introduced over the years at the national and provincial levels to govern the protection of natural and cultural heritage and the development of these sites. Yet there remains some important lacunas in the legal framework governing tourism resource utilization (Shao and Ruan 2002). Similarly, there is no appropriate concession framework to attract and guide different types of investment in tourism development. In particular, conflicts between resource protection and tourism development are evident at popular cultural heritage sites.

Leshan and Jiuzhaigou in Sichuan province are examples of this. Leshan is the location of one of the largest and oldest statues in the world, the 71 m-high Maitreya Buddha carved in a cliff along the Minjiang River during the Tang Dynasty (618–907 CE), while Jiuzhaigou is a formerly isolated mountain region

Fig. 5.4 Long Lake, Jiuzhaigou National Park, Sichuan province

in northern Sichuan that became one of the country's first national parks in 1982. During summer months, both sites receive as many as 30,000 visitors a day. Jiuzhaigou was among the first world heritage sites in China to introduce a modern digitized park management system designed to minimize human impact on the natural environment (Fig. 5.4). But in the face of rapidly rising number of visitors, the Jiuzhaigou Management Committee has acceded to local government and business pressure and repeatedly raised daily limits on the number of people allowed into the park, despite the fact that a maximum environmental carrying capacity of 28,000 daily visitors has been recommended by several impact studies (Wang and Yu 2007; Zhang and Zhu 2007; Qiu et al. 2010). The current level of visitation is causing serious concerns among environmental and tourism experts for its long-term consequence on Jiuzhaigou's unique ecological environment, as well as the enjoyment of visitors. In Leshan, visitors often have to stand in line for several hours to descend to the foot of the Giant Buddha via an ancient pathway, posing a threat to this cultural heritage site and to the safety of visitors.

It is also interesting to note that the concept of integrated development of a destination, not just a scenic site, has yet to be implemented by tourism management institutions in China. For instance, also in Sichuan, Mount Emei (E'meishan), one of Chinese Buddhism's four pilgrimage mountains, is located near E'meishan City, but the heritage site and the municipality are under two administrative systems with limited coordination. There is no integrated economic and tourism development plan, no unified strategy or management system, and no joint tourism promotion efforts. Although the mountain is now a national park, the city continues to lack basic infrastructure and service facilities. Moreover, despite the fact that Leshan and E'meishan are only 30 min apart and were jointly inscribed on the world heritage site list, these belong to separate administrative districts and scenic area management committees, with little communication in terms of their development strategies, management models, and marketing efforts and almost no substantive cooperation.

As indicated in the foregoing discussion, a large number of government agencies play an active role in the heritage tourism value chain, either as providers of public facilities and services or as regulators of service providers. Poorly coordinated tourism institutions with blurred responsibilities have led to the ineffective management of tourism development. China's current tourism administration faces two contradictory problems. On the one hand, central administrators are overburdened with too many functions that reflect a centrally planned economy, but at the same time, a fragmentation of bureaucratic authority has made effective and sustainable planning difficult. In addition, most heritage funding has become the responsibility of local governments, thereby limiting the influence of central actors.

The Admissions Economy Phenomenon

The Chinese government's decision to become a member party of the World Heritage Convention in 1985 signified a paradigm shift in domestic heritage management, from a focus on protecting cultural relics to an emphasis on cultural heritage conservation (Lü 2008). In 1987, UNESCO inscribed six Chinese sites on its world heritage list: the Forbidden City in Beijing, the Great Wall, the Zhoukoudian Peking Man Site, Mount Tai (Taishan) in Shandong province, the tomb of Emperor Qin Shi Huang and adjacent Terracotta Army near Xian, and the Mogao Caves in Dunhuang, Gansu province. The subsequent listing of 37 additional world heritage sites has contributed to the transfer of knowledge of heritage protection as well as restoration and management practices to Chinese heritage professionals. Examples of this are the digitized management system used by Jiuzhaigou National Park management in Sichuan province and the increasing use of GIS systems in the design of preservation plans for ancient villages (Hu and Dong 2003).

World heritage and national heritage status usually translate into increased visibility and tourism arrivals, stimulating local economic development. Two of the best known examples of this are the historical communities of Lijiang in Yunnan province and Pingyao in Shanxi province. In both cases, inscription on the world heritage list in 1997 generated tremendous economic and social impact. In Lijiang, for example, tourism arrivals are estimated to be as high as 7.4 million per year (Su and Teo 2009) (Fig. 5.5).

But the development and funding of most sites have contributed to an "admissions economy" phenomenon. Heritage destinations rely primarily on admissions revenues to support tourism development due to insufficient funding from the national and provincial governments as well as the lack of integration of tourism products and services. For example, reports indicate that the national government

Fig. 5.5   Street Scene, Lijiang, Yunnan province

only appropriates ¥10 million (approximately $1.6 million) annually for the
development and maintenance of China's 177 national-level scenic areas (Liu and
Yao 2011). Such budget funding is far from enough to operate and maintain these
cultural heritage sites. With little direct national financial assistance, most cultural
heritage sites have to rely on admission revenues to manage operations and maintain cultural heritage resources.

   One of the strategies used by local officials is to have sites or places of historical
significance approved as national "Protected Sites of Significant Cultural Relics"
and then petition to have these nominated for UNESCO world cultural heritage
status (Lü 2008). As of July 2012, the People's Republic had 43 sites on UNESCO's
world heritage list. An additional 52 sites have been nominated and remain on the
tentative list, while 36 others have been nominated in the past but have subsequently
been withdrawn, either because they were incorporated into other listings or failed
to receive preliminary approval from UNESCO authorities.

   In this drive to gain heritage standing, local government agencies have invested
in renovation projects or even the wholesale reconstruction of historical and cultural
sites. This of course runs counter to one of the core principles established by the
World Heritage Convention for selecting world cultural heritage sites: the authenticity of a cultural heritage site should be reflected in its original architectural form
with original building materials and building techniques (Ruan and Lin 2004).
Despite this prohibition, extensive reconstruction has occurred at both Pingyao and
Lijiang. In Pingyao, the city gate tower and city moat were completely rebuilt in

1998, while in Lijiang, the local government reconstructed several groups of wood houses in the old town in 1999 (Ruan and Lin 2003). This rebuilding of cultural heritage sites raises serious concerns about the integrity of cultural heritage since dominant transnational heritage norms insist that new construction cannot have the same value as the original.

In addition, admission prices for many national sites have risen dramatically in the last several decades, driven by local government development projects and because of the multiple government agencies with oversight authority that extract rents from ticket revenues. Admission prices are not set by a national agency, as in the United States with the National Park Service. Instead, fees vary by province, site, and season. For instance, admission to Jiuzhaigou National Park in Sichuan is currently ¥310 ($45.60) during the peak season from April 1 to November 15, which includes a mandatory ¥90 ($14) fee for shuttle service inside the park. This is reduced to ¥80 ($12.50) for admission and a further ¥80 for shuttle service during winter months.[1] The Qin Dynasty Terracotta Warrior Museum near Xian, Shaanxi province, charges ¥150 ($23.60) during the peak season and ¥120 ($18.85) during winter months.

Authorities justify these relatively high prices by stating that a portion of this money is earmarked for local communities. For instance, of the ¥168 ($26) admission fee for Mount Wutai (Wutai Shan) National Park and world heritage site in Shanxi province, a portion is in theory used to assist local residents who have been displaced by heritage development (see Chap. 6). More common is the direct transfer of some of these funds to local governments. For example, 40% of the admission fees for the Great Wall at Badaling Scenic Area (currently ¥45 per person) are handed over to the treasury of Yanqing County, where this portion of the Wall is located (Jiang 2010). Authorities also argue that increasing admission costs is an effective means of managing visitor totals, thereby contributing to heritage conservation efforts while sustaining heritage sites as revenue generators. Finally, supporters of this model also point out that iconic sites in easily accessible urban areas are either free (such as the National Museum of China and Tiananmen Square in Beijing, West Lake in Hangzhou, and the Bund in Shanghai) or have relatively low admission prices (such as the Forbidden City and Temple of Heaven in Beijing, Zhoukoudian (site of the Peking Man archeological dig), Kunming's Western Hills, and Shanghai's Jade Buddha Temple).[2]

---

[1] Half price admission is offered to students under the age of 18, retirees under the age of 70, Buddhist pilgrims who have official letters of introduction from their home province, and handicapped people. Admission is free for seniors over the age of 70 years, armed forces personnel, disabled veterans, and retired military personnel with special retirement privileges. Pricing for admissions to cultural heritage sites is often determined by provincial government agencies as well as from feedback from public hearings. For instance, the decision to offer discount admission for students was first made by the State Development and Reform Commission, although each provincial Development and Reform Commission sets the admission price for its own sites.

[2] Tickets for the Forbidden City cost ¥60 and the Temple of Heaven ¥35; Zhoukoudian, Kunming's Western Hills, and the Jade Buddha Temple cost ¥30.

Table 5.2 Admission costs for Yellow Mountain and its popular attractions (2012)

Site/attraction	Admission	Site/attraction	Admission
Yellow Mountain scenic area	¥232 (¥230admission+ ¥2 insurance)	Yu Ping cable car	¥80(one-way)/person
Yun Gu cable car (two lines)	¥80(one-way)/person	Tai Ping cable car	¥80(one-way)/person
Shuttle at Yellow Mountain scenic area	¥26/person	Hongcun (village) at Yi County	¥80/person
Xidi Village at Yi County	¥80/person	Tangmo Village in Huizhou	¥55/person
Nanping Village	¥30/person	Qiankou in Huizhou	¥50/person
Huashan Mysterious Grottoes	¥91/person	Jiulong Waterfall	¥42/person
Chengkan Village in Huizhou	¥35/person	Huangshan Ravishing Hotspring	¥128/person(regular) ¥180/person(VIP)
Feicui (Jade) Valley	¥70/person	Huangshan Hulinyuan (tiger reserve)	¥158/person
Huangshan Xiuning Giant Panda Ecological Park	¥180/person	Huangshan Furong Valley	¥98/person

Source: Huangshan Scenic Area Management Commission (2012)

Nevertheless, an increasing number of Chinese scholars have been critical of the high admission costs for most famous heritage sites, pointing out that in many cases these are higher than admission to US national parks, despite the substantial income gap between the two countries. Indeed, the World Bank has calculated that as of 2011, US GDP per capita was $48,450, compared to $5,430 in China (World Bank 2011). These critics argue that high admission costs have priced out many low-income people who should have the right to have access to national heritage sites (Zhou and Xiong 2010). They also reject the claim that increased admission pricing helps conservation efforts, pointing out that in China, no empirical evidence supports this assumption. For example, in a study of the impact of entrance fees on visitor arrivals to the country's most famous mountain, Yellow Mountain (Huangshan) Li (2005) found that, while ticket prices rose from ¥2 (approximately 25 cents) in 1986 to ¥132 ($21) in 2002, the number of annual tourists remained consistent at 1.2 million (Li 2005: 59). Obviously, pricing was not an effective economic tool to curb the number of tourists to this world heritage site. In 2009, the admission price to Huangshan was increased to ¥202 ($32) and in 2012 to ¥232 ($36), including ¥2 for insurance.[3] As steep as this price is, this entry ticket allows visitors to only tour the main heritage site. Shuttle bus services, a cable car, and popular scenic spots along the mountain all require additional tickets, as illustrated in Table 5.2.

---

[3] The listed admissions are for the peak season which covers March 1 to November 30. Off season is from December 1 to the end of February, when admission is reduced to ¥150. Discounted and free admissions are granted to various groups of the population.

In fact, far from declining in the face of steep price increases, tourist arrivals to Huangshan continue to show phenomenal growth. According to the China National Tourism Administration (CNTA), Huangshan received 30.54 million tourists in 2011, 96% of whom were domestic, generating ¥25.1 billion ($3.9 billion) in revenues. The number of tourist arrivals was 20.03% ahead of 2010, and the revenue increased by 27.91% over that of 2010 (CNTA 2012). The local government has set a goal of 35 million tourists in 2012, including 1.6 million foreigners, and ¥30 billion in revenues (CNTA 2012).

These figures demonstrate that tourism has clearly generated substantial inputs in the local economy. But of the total tourist revenues generated in 2011, how much actually was directed to the heritage site? According to the Director of Accounting in the Economic Development Office of the Huangshan Scenic Area Management Commission, ticket sales in 2011 generated ¥563 million in revenue for the management commission, 73.6% of which (¥413 million) was used for conservation efforts and routine maintenance (Wang and Tao 2012). This includes safeguarding ancient and famous trees and plants, trail repair programs, forest protection, forest fire prevention and pine wilt disease prevention, hygiene, sanitation, and waste management. The Huangshan Scenic Area Management Commission also received ¥23.36 million from various government agencies in 2011 for the conservation of heritage resources (Wang and Tao 2012). These government funds are not, however, fixed allocations. Instead, these are appropriated by specific agencies for specific purposes, such as funding from the provincial Bureau of Cultural Heritage for restoring a particular cultural object or building, or funding from the provincial Environmental Protection Agency for wastewater treatment.

The example of Huangshan illustrates a key financial challenge faced by heritage site managers. Even if a third of all visitors to this park benefited from reduced entry fees, total gross revenue from ticket sales likely exceeded ¥4 billion in 2011. Of this total, less than 15% was invested into the heritage site. And, of total revenues reported by the local government, just 1% was budgeted for conservation. This creates a circular dilemma: most heritage sites in China must depend on local funding, while local authorities often view heritage sites as revenue generators. Local government officials seek to maximize revenues by increasing the number of visitors to heritage sites, which puts more strain on existing conservation efforts and creates new conservation needs. But only a small percentage of the monies generated by admission fees are returned to site managers.

An alternative, of course, is for local authorities to contract site management to a private company, which in return provides fixed rents and is responsible for managing the site. But as we have seen, a desire to maximize profits will likely clash with the need for increased investments in heritage protection. A private model might well offer a more efficient management system, but this does not guarantee that public goods (in the form of heritage) will be protected.

Yet relying on local authorities to care for heritage sites also raises practical issues. As noted above, local officials may not worry about the long-term interests of a heritage site if they believe they will not be present to deal with potential

Table 5.3 Tourism development in Chengde after world heritage status and economic impact (1995–2011)

Year	Domestic arrivals				Overseas arrivals				
	Arrivals 000	% Change	Receipts million ¥	% Change	Arrivals 000	% Change	Receipts million $	% Change	%GDP
1995	1,931	–	580	–	81	–	3.61	–	2.33
1996	2,100	8.80	690	19	100	23.5	5.71	40.8	3.00
1997	2,520	20.00	800	15.9	110	10.1	7.16	25.5	6.06
1998	2,810	11.50	900	12.5	90	−18.2	7.15	0	5.99
1999	3,100	13.30	1,169	29.8	111.2	23.4	9.46	32.3	7.38
2000	3,550	10.00	1,200	12.5	127	11.0	11.51	15.5	8.09
2001	4,045	10.90	1,460	10.6	145	13.5	13.83	20.2	8.00
2002	4,709	20.70	1,870	28.4	158	9.0	15.42	11.5	10.00
2003	4,104	−12.9	1,730	−7	79.8	−49.5	7.85	−49.1	7.36
2004	5,351	30.38	2,191	26.65	169	112	16.8	114	7.77
2005	6,033	12.75	2,857	30.40	186	10.06	19.983	18.95	8.39
2006	6,806	12.81	3,504	22.65	215.5	15.86	47.02	135	9.11
2007	7,983	17.30	4,290	22.43	248	15.08	55.39	17.8	8.56
2008	7,345	−7.99	4,640	8.16	201	−18.95	58.66	5.9	7.08
2009	10,603	44.36	6,840	47.41	206	2.49	54.75	−6.7	9.45
2010	12,820	20.91	8,635	26.24	258	25.24	73.68	34.58	10.39
2011	16,676	30.08	11,883	37.61	312	20.93	110.75	50.31	11.45

Source: Bureau of Statistics, city of Chengde

negative consequences in the future. In addition, conservation efforts can clash not just with visitor quotas but also larger development programs.

The Qing Summer Resort in Chengde is a good example. Chengde, called Jehol before 1949, is a relatively small city of 450,000 located in Hebei province, 230 km north of Beijing. After it was selected by the Kang Xi Emperor as the site of a royal summer retreat in 1703, an elaborate park was built along with a collection of Buddhist temples. The resulting complex of more than 120 buildings served as the second political center in the Qing Dynasty after Beijing, where Emperor Kang Xi and Emperor Qianlong managed state affairs. The resort was listed as one of the first 24 famous historical and cultural cities in China and one of the country's top ten 10 scenic areas (Qi et al. 2007). Chengde was also inscribed as a world cultural heritage site in December 1994, in the second group of Chinese cultural heritage sites approved by UNESCO. Since then, Chengde has experienced significant tourism development as seen in Table 5.3 (Fig. 5.6).

Domestic tourism increased annually between 1995 and 2011, except for 2003 during the SARS scare and 2008, the year of the Beijing Olympic Games. Annual domestic arrivals reached 10 million in 2009 and jumped to 16.68 million in 2011. However, international arrivals have been relatively flat, reaching 312,000 in 2011, or less than 2% of total arrivals. Clearly, Chengde, as is the case for arguably every world heritage site in China, is primarily popular with domestic tourists. Economically, tourism's contribution to the local GDP increased from 2.33% in 1995 to 11.45% in 2011.

Fig. 5.6 Nine-story pagoda (built in 1751), Qing Imperial Mountain Resort, Chengde, Hebei province

City planners have aggressive development plans for future growth as an international tourism destination. The city government allocated ¥4.6 billion in 2010 to relocate residents near the royal summer palace and the various temples in the area. This resettlement project is the largest ever undertaken in Chengde and will eventually move 15,000 residents of 5,400 households as well as 36 state-owned and private businesses (Li 2012). The cleared land from demolished houses and business buildings is estimated at 1.3 million square meters. The city plans to develop a new commercial center for tourism services using part of the newly cleared land. In 2011, the central government also provided a special allocation of ¥600 million (approximately $80 million) for the conservation of the royal summer palace and the temples and construction of service facilities.

However, this relocation project will not return the heritage site to its original form. Instead, city leaders have much bigger plans in mind for further economic development using heritage tourism as the engine. The secretary of the city's Communist Party Committee has explained the purpose of the relocation project as "using the vacated space as the center of cultural tourism service development and paving the foundation for promoting an international tourism city" (quoted in Liang et al. 2012). This plan involves not just the conservation of existing heritage resources but the creation of a heritage-like destination. In fact, the director of Chengde's Municipal Tourism Administration has stated that the city government will invest ¥8.7 billion to develop a new summer resort palace that mirrors the original royal summer palace and will be a new iconic landmark, thereby attracting even more tourists (Li 2012). Obviously, more tourists will bring more revenues to the city and will continue to make up a greater share of the local GDP.

In summary, the Chinese government's decision to decentralize both governance decisions and funding to provincial and local authorities has affected heritage management in multiple ways. Local officials tend to view heritage sites as sources of revenue, not as public goods to protect and preserve. In cases such as Chengde, a national heritage site may become the foundation of an elaborate local economic development project.

Finally, decentralization also significantly impacts future heritage sites. National heritage regulations place responsibility for protecting new archeological findings on local authorities, who are also expected to emphasize economic development. Quite predictably, development projects may lead to the discovery of artifacts in the course of construction. For example, 21 Shang Dynasty bronze artifacts from the eleventh century BCE were recently discovered in a village in Shaanxi province while workers were digging a foundation (*China Daily* June 26 2012).

Under current laws, if any material artifacts are uncovered during construction projects, these must be protected, using local funds. If a site is discovered on private property, the owner is responsible for its protection (Svensson 2006: 30). Thus, local governments do not necessarily welcome potential new heritage sites because of the costs involved in protection (Gruber 2007: 182). And, because local officials are evaluated and promoted largely on their success in promoting economic growth, they have little incentive to fund preservation programs unless a site has potential as a tourist attraction (Li et.al. 2008: 309).

Bibliography

Agnew, Neville, and Martha Demas (eds.). 2004. *Principles for the conservation of heritage in China.* Los Angeles: The Getty Conservatory Institute.

Bai, Zhang. 2004. Afterword. In *Principles for the conservation of heritage in China*, ed. Neville Agnew and Martha Demas, 91–93. Los Angeles: The Getty Conservatory Institute.

Chen, Shen, and Hong Chen. 2010. Cultural heritage management in China: Current practices and problems. In *Cultural heritage management: A global perspective*, ed. Phyllis Messenger and George Smith, 70–81. Gainsville: University of Florida.

China Daily. 2012. 11th century BC bronze ware found, June 26. http://usa.chinadaily.com.cn/epaper/2012-06/26/content_15523288.htm. Accessed 31 July 2012.

China National Tourism Administration. 2012. The City of Huangshan strives to receive 1.6 million overseas tourists in 2012. http://www.cnta.gov.cn/html/2012-2/2012-2-9-14-48-89289.html. Accessed 14 July 2012.

China National Tourism Office (CNTO). 2008. Major statistics of Chinese tourism, Jan–Dec 2008. http://www.cnta.gov.cn/html/2009-2/2009-2-18-9-34-95871.html. Accessed 10 Oct 2011.

China National Tourism Office (CNTO). 2009. Foreign visitor arrivals by purpose, Jan–Dec 2009. http://cnto.org/chinastats_2009ArrivalsByPurpose.asp. Accessed 12 Oct 2011.

Chun, Qi, Dong Jin, and Peng Hongbin. 2007. Strategic analysis of developing international tourism in Chengde. *Modern Economy* 6(6): 252–255.

Gruber, Stefan. 2007. Protecting China's cultural heritage sites in times of rapid change. *Asian Pacific Journal of Environment and Law* 253(10): 253–301.

He, Huang. 2004. Consideration on non-state enterprise's involvement in development of scenery spots – The model of Bifeng valley. *Journal of Yibin University* 2(2): 58–60.

Huixian, Shen. 2011. Research on the risks of scenic area management of state ownership and private operations. *Commercial Economics* 5: 56–58.

Ji, Li. 2005. Questioning the economics of admission increases by world heritage sites. *Journal of Liaoning Provincial College of Communications* 7(4): 58–59. 73.

Kuili, Liu. 2007. On issues concerning culturally ecological reserves. *Journal of Zhejiang Normal University* 32(3): 9–12.

Li Mimi, Wu Bihu and Cai Liping. 2008. "Tourism Development of Heritage Sites in China." *Tourism Management* 29: 308–319.

Li Min. 2012. Chengde summer palace: Highlight tourism cultural attractions and create a city landmark. *HSDNEWS*, July 9. http://www.hsdnews.cn/news/2012-07/09/c_112387424.htm. Accessed 17 July 2012.

Liang Shifang, Guo Feng, and Li Jiancheng. 2012. Chengde city, Hebei province, creates new support for developing and targeting high-end international-quality tourist city. *HSDNEWS*, July 3. http://www.hsdnews.cn/news/2012-07/03/c_112343414.htm. Retrieved 17 July 2012.

Lijie, Zhou, and Xiong Liming. 2010. On the 'Admissions Economy' of chaotic ticket price hikes and control. *Consumer Economic* 26(1): 66–69.

Liu Jingsong. 2012. Shao Lin temple, the platform for fame and fortune. *Economic Observation Press*, December 21.

Mingxing, Hu, and Dong Wei. 2003. Management information system of vernacular village protection based on GIS. *Engineering Journal of Wuhan University* 36(3): 53–56.

Mingzhu, Liang, Bao Chunxiao, and Xu Xiaoqian. 2009. Protection and development situation of world heritage in the national scenic interest areas and international experience study. *Economic Geography* 29(1): 141–146.

Ministry of Housing and Urban–rural Development. 2010 and 2012. Awarding the seventh group of national scenic areas. http://www.mohurd.gov.cn/zxydt/201001/t20100128_199489.html. Retrieved 25 July 2012.

Nyiri, Pal. 2006. *Scenic spots: Chinese tourism, the state, and cultural authority.* Seattle: University of Washington.

Peng Xiang. 2001. The current situation, cause of formation and countermeasures of the environmental problems in Wulingyuan scenic spot. *Tourism Tribune.* http://en.cnki.com.cn/Article_en/CJFDTotal-LYXK200001014.htm. Retrieved 19 Aug 2012

Qifu, Wu, and Wang Ruhui. 2007. Review of research on the old town of Lijiang – The world cultural heritage. *Tourism Science* 21(1): 17–21.

Rui, Jiang. 2010. On reforming tourism scenic area classification and management in China. *Market Modernization* December: 51–52.

Runa, Yisan, and Lin Lin. 2004. Authenticity in relation to the conservation of urban cultural heritage. *Urban and Rural Development* 4: 29–30.

Shaoli, Xu, Xi Jianchao, and Xiao Jianyong. 2006. Five premises on rope way construction at tourist scenic spots. *Area Research and Development* 25(6): 80–82. 103.

Shepherd, Robert. 2012. *Faith in heritage: Displacement, development, and religious tourism in contemporary China.* Walnut Grove: Left Coast Press.

Sichuan Travel and Tourism Administration. 2012. The twelfth five-year plan for scenic area development and world heritage in Sichuan province. Chengdu: Sichuan Travel & Tourism Administration.

Sofield, Trevor, and Fung Mei Li. 1998. Tourism development and cultural policies in China. *Annals of Tourism Research* 25(2): 362–392.

State Administration of Cultural Heritage. 2006 and 2012. Announcements on the verification of national important cultural heritage sites. http://www.sach.gov.cn/tabid/96/InfoID/60/frtid/134/Default.aspx. Retrieved 25 July 2012.

Su Xiaobo & Peggy Teo. 2009. *The Politics of Heritage Tourism in China: a View from Lijiang.* London: Routledge.

Svensson, Marina. 2006. *In the ancestor's shadow: Cultural heritage contestations in Chinese villages*. Working Paper #16. Stockholm: Centre for East and Southeast Asian Studies, Lund University.

Wang Liwu, and Tao Ye. 2012. First response by Huangshan scenic area management commission: 70% of admission revenues are used for world heritage conservation. http://news.xinhuanet.com/2012-04/09/c_111752042.htm?finance. Retrieved 14 July 2012.

Weller, Robert. 2006. *Discovering nature: Globalization and environmental culture in China and Taiwan*. Cambridge: Cambridge University Press.

World Bank. 2012. *World Development Indicators (WDI) and Global Development Finance (GDF)*. Washington, DC: The World Bank. http://databank.worldbank.org/ddp/home.do?Step=12&id=4&CNO=2. Accessed 30 July 2012.

Xiao, Zhang, and Zhen Yuqian. 2001. *The management of China's natural and cultural heritage resources*. Beijing: Social Science Archive Press.

Xiaoan, Wei. 2000. Reflecting on listing companies managing tourism scenic area on the equity market. *Tourism Tribute* 1: 73–75.

Xiaobo, Li. 2002. Business operation system reform and its problems of Sichuan scenic resorts. *Journal of Sichuan Normal University (Social Science Section)* 29(3): 113–117.

Xiaobo, Su, and Peggy Teo. 2009. *The politics of heritage tourism in China: A view from Lijiang*. London: Routledge.

Xie, Chensheng. 2002. Five decades of cultural relics protection in New China. *Contemporary Chinese History Studies* 9(3): 61–70.

Xingbin, Wang. 2002. The reform of managerial modes of China's natural and cultural heritage. *Tourism Tribute* 17(5): 15–21.

Xu, Songling. 2003. On reforming China's cultural and natural heritage management system. *Management World* 6: 63–73.

Xu, Songling. 2005. On the significance of Bifengxia tourist development pattern. *Journal of Sichuan Normal University (Social Science Edition)* 32(1): 41–47.

Xuelei, Liu, and Yao Guorong. 2011. Reasons and policy research in price increase of admissions to tourist attraction. *Journal of Hebei Tourism Vocational College* 16(4): 53–57.

Yanqing, Qiu, Ge Peng, and Ren Peiyu. 2010. A study of temporal and spatial navigation based on the load-balance of tourists in Jiuzhaigou valley. *Resources Science* 32(1): 118–123.

Yiping, Li. 2003. Heritage tourism: The contradictions between conservation and change. *Tourism and Hospitality Research* 4(3): 247–261.

Yisan, Runa, and Lin Lin. 2003. Authenticity in relation to the conservation of cultural heritage. *Tongji University Journal Social Science Section* 14(2): 1–5.

Yong, Wang, and Yu Sujun. 2007. Environmental capacity investigation of Jiuzhaigou scenic spot. *Sichuan Environment* 26(2): 17–22.

Yong, Shao, and Ruan Yisan. 2002. On the legal framework for the protection of historical and cultural heritage. *Journal of Urban Planning* 3: 57–60. 65.

Zhang, Xiaoping, and Zhu Zhongfu. 2007. An analysis to tourism capacity in Jiuzhaigou scenic area. *Tourism Tribune* 22(9): 50–57.

Zhou, Lü. 2008. Thirty-years of cultural heritage protection in China. *Conservation of Architectural Heritage* 12: 1–5.

Chapter 6
The Social Impact of Heritage

As previously noted, after 1949, cultural institutions such as museums, schools, religious buildings and, at the village level, ancestral halls and other spiritual sites were closely regulated or seized by the new authorities. The goal immediately after the establishment of the People's Republic was not to preserve the past for its own sake but to utilize this to help shape a new socialist collective identity. In support of this party project to cultivate socialist citizens, the peasantry was organized first into collectives and later into communes, and urban residents into work units (*danwei*). In the latter, all the needs of its members were met behind the walls of each unit, making these both the primary social web and a foundational aspect of members' identity. The goal was to create a micro-society that simultaneously displaced preferential kin ties and turned social relationships into a key aspect of production (Bray 2005: 96). In doing so, public (*gong*) and private (*si*) distinctions were transformed, as "state" and "public" were collapsed into a single category, and the private sphere was erased. The result was the replacement of public-private distinctions, in the form of kin and other, with a lived form of public life that contrasted with an abstract general public – the public/state space of the nation (Lu and Perry 1997: 10; Womack 1991: 324).

It would, however, be a mistake to reduce work units to either the most visible form of an all-powerful state or the site of potential resistance to central authority. Until the 1990s, personal identity was grounded in work units. Work units thus

---

In this final chapter, we examine the impact archeological and cultural heritage projects have on contemporary social relationships and the ways in which local communities respond to such projects. While heritage preservation often is presented as socially beneficial, how this affects local communities depends on a number of factors. The location of sites (urban versus rural), the role of ethnicity (Han Chinese versus an officially recognized minority group), the importance different state authorities place on a site, and above all the approaches of local authorities to management issues lead to different outcomes. Heritage preservation has created new destinations for tourists and new opportunities for Chinese citizens to learn about their country's history and culture. But it has also resulted in displacement of local residents, destruction of material culture, and the construction of commercialized heritage destinations divorced from any actual historical context.

R.J. Shepherd and L. Yu, *Heritage Management, Tourism, and Governance in China: Managing the Past to Serve the Present*, SpringerBriefs in Archaeology 2, DOI 10.1007/978-1-4614-5918-7_6, © Springer Science+Business Media, LLC 2013

served as a distinct form of society, distinct from both "society" and "the state" (Lu and Perry 1997: 12). In other words, European liberal distinctions between state and society as well as individuals and the state made little sense in this context. Instead, individual identity was shaped and constrained by work unit identity, which in turn both shaped and constrained notions of "society."

As Womack (1991) has noted, many discussions of the totalitarian power of the Chinese state under Mao tend to assume a state-citizen template of social order, thus ignoring the actual complexities of a work unit-rooted society. The standard critique of work unit society accepts as a given both the liberal concept of autonomous individual citizens and what follows from this, an assumption that a social order based on collective institutions would automatically *not* be attractive to individuals, because it binds them socially to employers. It follows from this that workers in a market economy are freer because employers can only fire them from their jobs, not penalize their access to housing, education, food, and other necessities (1991: 321–322). However, these assumptions only hold true if work unit administrators actually were able to utilize this power. In fact, it was often quite difficult to dismiss someone completely from a work unit. Moreover, this perspective assumes that material and job security accompanied by severe restrictions on personal freedoms will not be acceptable to all people, which again may well not be true in practice.

After 1979, state rhetoric shifted from revolutionary socialism to modernization and development. During the reform period, agricultural land has been parceled out to peasants on leasehold agreements, and most urban work units have been hallowed out, their housing stock sold to members and services outsourced. For members of work units in desirable cities or neighborhoods, these reforms have created much wealth as housing prices have soared. But for members of work units in less desirable cities or industries that have not adapted, these market reforms have destroyed their livelihoods.

Economic reforms also necessitated a loosening of state control of people's mobility, as new export-oriented industries demanded a large supply of cheap labor. The result has been the creation of a new laboring class of as many as 200 million mobile peasants who fill low-wage factory and construction jobs (Lee 2007). But in addition to this marginalized class of exploited peasants, the reforms have created a relatively small but growing class of citizens with disposable income and a desire to travel.

In 1998 tourism was officially defined as a key growth area of the national economy, in part to encourage domestic consumer demand during the Asian financial crisis of 1998 and 1999 (Nyiri 2009: 153). By 2007, the number of domestic tourists (1.6 billion, measured by total trips) far outnumbered foreign arrivals (130 million). And, of the latter, approximately 80% (105.8 million) were ethnic Chinese residents of Hong Kong, Taiwan, and Macau. Only 8.7 million were from the European Community and the United States (CNTA 2008, 2009).

China today is a country in which two groups have become mobile: a marginalized peasant class of factory hands, construction workers, nannies, street vendors, and other marginal occupations that increasingly affluent urban residents no longer want to do, and an emerging urban consumer class with the disposable income and leisure time to tour. This unprecedented peacetime movement of citizens has fueled

Fig. 6.1 Tour group waiting to enter the Forbidden City, Beijing, 2010

the heritage industry and has enabled millions to experience places and sites their parents could only have imagined (Fig. 6.1). But this mass movement of people has also created an enormous demand for tourist destinations, which has translated into a renewed state interest in heritage. While local communities have been allowed to reclaim their (collective) pasts, the material basis of this has increasingly been redefined by government officials as "cultural heritage." In theory, local communities are key stakeholders in decision making about heritage projects. However, due to China's complex administrative and bureaucratic structures as well as different types and scales of cultural heritage projects, this is not always the case. The net result often is a loss of agency at the community level, not (as in the recent past) in the service of revolution but in the name of (economic) development (Svensson 2006).

The Paradox of Heritage Preservation

As noted in Chap. 4, UNESCO, the World Union of Conservation, and associated transnational heritage organizations promote a spatial plan for heritage organization and management that divides protected areas into separate zones, ranging from an inner core to an outer fringe area (Weller 2006: 78). This global model, which is supposed to strengthen cultural diversity, may paradoxically have the opposite effect, transforming world heritage sites into remarkably similar spatial zones while displacing local residents in the name of preservation (Shepherd 2012).

In China, this model has been closely followed. For example, the original intent in designating national scenic areas beginning in the 1980s was to replicate the national park system model found in Europe and the United States. This is reflected in the English translation of national scenic areas (*guojia fengjing qu*) as "National Parks of China" and reflects underlying cultural assumptions about the separation of natural and cultural spaces. However, most of these scenic areas are a blend of natural landscapes and cultural heritage, such as Mount Wutai (Wutai Shan) in Shanxi province, Yellow Mountain (Huangshan) in Anhui province, and the West Lake (Xihu) in Hangzhou, Zhejiang province, and include communities of long standing. In contrast, parks in Europe and North America are public places devoid of permanent settlements (although many were inhabited before they were categorized as parks). Whether in urban areas such as Washington, DC's Rock Creek Park or New York's Central Park or in rural national parks such as Yellowstone in Montana or Zion in Utah, a park is, by definition, a place where nature, not culture, is found. In this sense, these spaces exist not just as repositories of nature but also as culture's opposite. Americans thus go to parks to "get in touch with" or "go back to" nature.

But in China, many heritage sites that have been designated national or provincial parks have never been natural spaces completely separated from society. This is especially the case for sacred mountains, be these Buddhist sites such as Wutai Shan, Daoist sites like Huashan in Shaanxi province, or iconic imperial destinations such as Mount Tai (Taishan) in Shandong province. Instead, because these mountains have been pilgrimage sites for many centuries, a service economy has been the norm, overlapping with a religious service economy that has met the needs of devotees and resident religious personnel. This resulted in social spaces that blurred the boundaries between sacred and profane; public and private; religion and business; and above all, heritage and its suspect other, a world of commerce.

Despite this reality, to achieve UNESCO recognition for sites such as these and the cachet this credential carries in the marketing of heritage as a development resource, planners have had to meet the expectations of the dominant transnational heritage protection model: preservation through spatial segregation. The result has been the displacement of local residents, not only in the name of economic development as is so often the case in urban China, but also in the cause of heritage preservation. For example, the master plan for Mount Wutai separates this national park into four zones, ranging from a core conservation zone to a service zone located at the park boundaries (GOC 2008a: 240–241). The town of Taihuai, the main settlement in the region and home to dozens of small businesses, is included in the core conservation zone. Most residents will be resettled in a newly built town (Jingangku) located just inside the park's south gate 20 km from Taihuai, while 36 guesthouses and 108 shops will be demolished in the core zone and tourist facilities relocated to a new service complex, also near the south gate (GOC 2008b: 288). A tourist reception center, Buddhist museum, shopping complex, and a five-star resort are also being built in the same area. When the plan is fully implemented in 2025, the inner zone of the Mount Wutai National Park will consist of monasteries, temples, gardens, and forests. The local community will have been eradicated and resettled approximately 20 km away. While residents have already engaged in small-scale protests about

Fig. 6.2 Dozens of local homes were demolished in Taihuai, Mount Wutai, after the area became a national park and a world heritage site in 2010

compensation rates and the loss of their farmland and businesses, planners insist that they will benefit from better housing, education opportunities, and interaction with visitors, leading them to value cultural heritage (Ibid, 215) (Fig. 6.2).

The Wutai case demonstrates that local communities may have little input into heritage plans, despite the fact that local residents are usually the people most directly affected by these projects. This example also illustrates the ambiguity of the term "stakeholder." In this particular case, local residents are divided over compensation rates and the question of who actually is local and thus should receive resettlement funds. Meanwhile, another part of the local community, monks and monastic officials, stand to benefit from this plan. Once fully implemented, only religious practitioners will be able to stay inside the boundaries of the core conservation zone. Consequently, most of the major monasteries in and around Taihuai are engaging in a flurry of new construction, mainly of dormitories and guest quarters. At least in this case, a plan designed to strictly enforce material preservation by eliminating commercial enterprises has led to not preservation but construction, enriched religious institutions by effectively providing these with a monopoly on heritage business, and violated the property rights of secular residents.

Yet from the national state perspective in China, local stakeholders are already part of the heritage process. Governance, revenues, and budgets have all been decentralized since 1998, which has resulted in heritage preservation and development projects promoted by local officials. The problem is that from the state perspective, local officials reflect the desires of local communities, which, as the Wutai example shows, may often be untrue.

Fig. 6.3 The "New Qianmen," looking north toward the front gate to the Forbidden City, Beijing, 2011

Creating Heritage

A similar form of displacement has become the norm in urban areas as well, motivated not by heritage preservation but by commercial projects aimed at heritage construction. Beijing's Qianmen district, located just south of Tiananmen Square, was leveled as part of the city's redevelopment plans for the 2008 Olympics and rebuilt as a historical district by the SOHO Corporation, one of the city's largest property developers (Fig. 6.3). During the Qing Dynasty, Qianmen, already an important commercial district, flourished as the center of Beijing opera, as a home for scholars and artists, and as the city's main entertainment district. After liberation in 1949, the area's courtyard homes were divided up into quarters for workers. Then, beginning in 2005, hundreds of courtyard homes in the area's signature *hutong* (alleys) were demolished, and their residents displaced to the city's outer suburbs, while the main avenue was transformed into a pedestrian shopping mall (Yardley 2006). Qianmen today is a new type of entertainment district, one in which the actual history of the place has been eradicated while the space itself has been historicized (Layton 2007). This, however, is a sanitized historical snapshot of a nostalgic turn-of-the-century Beijing, a city caught between the end of the Qing Dynasty and the establishment of the People's Republic. This snapshot is less of a selected image of old Qianmen as it is an imagined place that ignores the area's history as a center of prostitution, opium dens, and gambling during this period, as well as the socialist housing policies of the 1950s (ibid).

Fig. 6.4 Xintiandi, Shanghai: once a working class neighborhood, now a trendy entertainment district

Thus, the "Qianmen model" for urban redevelopment involves not just the removal of current residents and a subsequent elimination of the space of everyday life, it also requires the cleaning up of history. This is as much in response to market logic as it is to Communist Party demands for a party-vetted historical message. Indeed, the same commercially driven sanitization of the past is found at many American festive marketplaces, such as Faneuil Hall in Boston and Alexandria, Virginia's Old Town (where the last lynching took place in 1921), as well as urban entertainment districts, such as the Gaslight district in San Diego or Washington, DC's former Chinatown.

The redevelopment of Shanghai's Xintiandi neighborhood, an area in the city center filled with *shikumen* houses, is an instructive example. This project predates Qianmen, having been initiated in 1997 as a joint venture between the Shanghai Municipal Government and Hong Kong's Shui On Property Group. US planners were hired to develop a commercial center that utilized the neighborhood's existing architecture (Chen 2007). The result has been, from one perspective, a transformation of a rundown area into a commercially successful entertainment district, one which has been internationally recognized for its innovative use of conservation principles, including by the United States Land Institute in 2003 (ibid). But from a different perspective, Xintiandi symbolizes the class divide at the heart of many heritage projects in urban China: a residential neighborhood remade as a commercial center for elites, far beyond the means of everyday citizens, especially those who once called it home (Fig. 6.4).

Similar urban development projects have been carried out in dozens of Chinese cities, from Datong and Hohhot in the east to Kunming in the west. But the most controversial of these projects is taking place in Kashgar, an ancient Silk Road city located in China's far west province of Xinjiang, near the Tajik border. Under the guise of eliminating unsafe housing and improving public safety, as much as 85% of the city's ancient quarter, inhabited by Uighurs, is scheduled to be demolished and replace with commercial enterprises and apartment blocks, with a small section to be restored as an outdoor heritage space (Hammer 2010). Despite local opposition and pleas from ICOMOS (2011), UNESCO, and the European Parliament (Global Heritage Fund 2011), more than 50% of the targeted area had been demolished by early 2012. This example illustrates how local governance efforts to generate revenue through commercial real estate partnerships at times intersect with national political objectives aimed at tempering minority aspirations, with devastating effect for the latter.

Development Versus Heritage

Finally, perhaps the most publicized aspect of heritage projects in China are trade-offs with large-scale development projects such as the construction of the massive Three Gorges Dam, the largest hydroelectric dam in the world. As one of the top national scenic areas in China, the Three Gorges area stretches 204 km along the Yangzi River, from Baidicheng in the west to Nanjinguan in the east (Tang 1998; Jiang et al. 2009). Completed in 2009, this 16-year mega infrastructure project costs approximately $30 billion and impacted 153 cities and towns, 1,352 villages, and 1,600 factories (Aird 2001). Raising the water level in the river basin completely submerged eight counties, nearly submerged another, and partially submerged four more (Zhuang 1999; Peng 2010). The project has displaced an estimated 1.3 million local residents and resulted in widespread cultural heritage destruction, particularly to more than 1,300 archeological sites dating back to the Warring States period (475–221 BCE) (Grubber 2007: 279–280).

While often attributed to Mao Zedong, the idea of a massive dam along the upper Yangzi to control flooding was first raised by Sun Yat-sen in an article published in 1919. In 1946, the Republic of China government signed an agreement with the United States Bureau of Reclamation for a dam project in the Three Gorges area, but work never began because of the Chinese Civil War (Ponseti and López-Pujol 2006: 153). The government of the People's Republic decided to move forward with such a project in 1954 in reaction to flooding that killed 30,000 people in the region. But political upheavals delayed this project until after Mao's death in 1976. The project was further delayed due to widespread domestic opposition among environmentalists, engineers, and notably, delegates to the National People's Congress. This led the Chinese People's Political Consultative Committee (NPPCC), usually a rubber stamp political body, to publicly demand a suspension of the project. In April 1992, dam construction was finally approved by the National People's Congress

(China's parliament) by a vote of 1,767–177 with 664 abstentions, meeting the two-thirds requirement by just 12 votes (Beattie 2002).

This project has generated heated debates between proponents and opponents both at home and abroad concerning its impact on the national economy, local people, cultural heritage, and the environment. The primary purposes of the dam are to generate electricity to meet the country's development needs, control flooding, and provide better navigation. Supporters argue that the hydropower generated by the dam is critical to China's continued economic development and attempt to shift away from its dependence on coal as an energy source. This is a critical environmental issue because most of the coal burned in China for energy use is soft coal, which is extremely polluting. Supporters note that the 100 annual megawatts of power that will eventually be produced by the dam would require 60 million tons of coal (Ponseti and López-Pujol 2006: 171). However, to this point, the power plants that have gone on-line produce only 4% of the country's electricity needs, which may not justify the cost of the total project. Moreover, increased sediment accumulation (a side effect of dam production) likely will dramatically reduce this output within a few years.

To improve flood control and provide greater navigation access, the dam has raised the water level of the Yangzi from 48.5 to 175 m (Li and Ye 2001). This is designed to control flooding that has been a problem for centuries. For example, more than 240,000 people died as a result of flooding in 1870, 145,000 in 1931, and 142,000 in 1935 (Ponseti and López-Pujol 2006: 161). Clearly, trying to control natural disasters such as this is a positive state goal. But the extent to which the Three Gorges project can control flooding in the lower Yangzi is open to question, particularly catastrophic events such as those cited by dam supporters (ibid, 163).

Finally, improved navigation will, supporters argue, lower transportation costs between inner China and the east coast and boost tourism in the region. It will also provide local residents with better housing and a new means of livelihood, tourism.

The State Administration of Cultural Heritage (SACH) was given overall authority to identify and move historical and cultural relics in the affected area. A heritage protection plan approved by the State Council identified 364 aboveground cultural heritage items for protection: 169 to be archived in museums, 135 to be relocated, and 61 to remain in situ (Shu and Chen 2010). Overall, 1,282 artifacts were reportedly identified and inventoried in areas to be submerged (Tang 1998; Li 1999).

Project supporters argue that the most important cultural heritage sites have been moved and protected, flooding has been controlled, and the dam as well as the new cities built for displaced people has become a major tourist attraction. But critics point out that only 1% of heritage sites were rescued before affected areas were fully submerged and, of this material, much has been relocated in "cultural parks" designed as tourist attractions (Le Mentec 2006: 1–2). Moreover, the most lasting harm has been to archeological sites, some of which date back to the Neolithic period. In many cases, lacking funding, archeological teams could only document sites before these were flooded.

Arguably the most jarring impact of this project was on residents displaced from their homes, work, fields, and collective past. What Le Mentec (2006) has termed the "trauma of upheaval" has not only divorced people from their own history, it has enabled local authorities to decide what counts as "heritage" by, for example, transforming worship sites into reconstructed tourist attractions. This is what has happened to the Zhang Fei Temple, the largest and costliest (an estimated $11 million) heritage site to be relocated. The temple, built during the Northern Song era (960–1,127 CE) to honor the famous general of the Three Kingdoms period (220–280 C), has been relocated from near Yunyang County in Sichuan to New Yunyang, 32 km upstream (Ponseti and López-Pujol 2006: 175). The new site lacks the aura of the original location, requires admission tickets, and strictly limits local worship practices (Le Mentec 2006: 6).

Becoming a Tourist Attraction

In addition to displacement in the name of national development, urban renewal, or heritage preservation, local residents often must grapple with crowds of visitors that radically transform everyday life and lead to economic displacement. The listing of Lijiang in 1997 as a world heritage site has transformed this small city in northern Yunnan province into one of the most popular tourism destinations in China. Lijiang, situated near the junction of Yunnan, Sichuan, and the Tibetan Autonomous Region (TAR), was a flourishing trade center on the ancient Silk Route and capital of the Naxi Kingdom. In 2000, Lijiang received 2.58 million domestic and overseas tourists who pumped a total of ¥1.344 billion (approximately $210 million) into the local economy. The popularity of this city has led to a "Lijiang Model" emulated by other local governments who want to leverage world heritage status to drive tourism development (Liu 2005). However, the gradual transformation of the social and cultural fabric of this ancient city has been documented in several studies (Liu 2005; Huang et al. 2009; Wu and Wang 2007). Liu (2005) analyzed the transformation of local economic and social networks in the old town, where the streets are lined with buildings that serve as both businesses and residences. These traditional buildings have a shop front and living quarters in an interior courtyard. After Lijiang was listed as a world heritage site, many traditional dwellings in the old town have been replaced by hotels, inns, restaurants, and bars. Of the 6,269 households living in the old town in 2001, an estimated 1,300 were engaged in tourism businesses. As more tourism service facilities have been set up in the old town, many retail shops that served local Naxi residents have disappeared. Now residents must commute to suburban areas even to buy daily necessities (Liu 2005).

Tourism has also significantly impacted human relationships in this community. As tourism arrivals have continued to rise, more and more local Naxi residents have leased their homes to outside business people and moved to new housing estates outside the city. Retail shops catering to local residents have continued to decrease since their profit margin is much lower than for tourism products (Huang et al. 2009). By 2004, 75% of retail shops in the central Si Fang Street area were tourist related, and only 39.5% were owned and operated by local residents. Moreover, less than

20% of residents in the old town were the original Naxi residents, with the remainder primarily from other parts of Yunnan province, Fujian, and Sichuan (Huang et al. 2009). This illustrates the "hollowing phenomenon" (*kongxinhuan*), a term used by Chinese scholars to describe the flight of the original residents of core heritage sites and the influx of outside business people taking residence in core heritage sites.

This influx of outside merchants to Lijiang has also threatened the sustainability of the traditional handicrafts made by Naxi residents. For instance, Naxi artisans have long been famous for their exquisitely crafted copperware. Now these products are copied and mass-produced elsewhere at a low cost and with shoddy workmanship and shipped to Lijiang for sale to tourists. Because they cannot compete with the low cost and fast production of these replicas, many local craftsmen have given up their trade (Liu 2005).

On the other hand, Thapa (2010) argues against any clear link between world heritage status and increased tourist arrivals at heritage sites. Using Lijiang as an example, he asserts that the sharp increase in visitor arrivals has been a result of improved access (by both road and air) and state policies aimed at boosting domestic tourism (282). This may well be true, but improved access alone does not make a site a tourist attraction. Moreover, whether millions of people now vacation in Lijiang because of its world heritage fame or for other reasons is beside the point: the social and cultural impact has been significant, as what was until recently the nexus of Naxi culture has been remade into a tourism-dominated commercial center populated mainly by outsiders. As Gruber (2007) notes, "it is sad and ironic that the originality and traditional ways of Lijiang are feared to disappear because the town has become a tourist attraction" (286).

World heritage status also has had a significant impact on residents of rural heritage sites. The historic villages of Xidi and Hongcun in Yi County, Anhui province, were inscribed on the UNESCO list in November 2000. Xidi, founded in 1047 CE, has three ancient ancestral halls, one decorated archway and 124 old folk houses from the Ming and Qing Dynasties. The village occupies an area of 16 ha and has a population of 1,070. Hongcun, founded in 1131, possesses two ancestral halls, one decorated archway, one school building, and 99 old folk dwellings from the Ming and Qing Dynasties. Hongcun has a total area of 24 ha and a population of 1,215 (Jin 2008). These cultural features quickly became the key development focus for county officials (Yuan et al. 2012; Li and Zhang 2006). Subsequently, heritage tourism has had a significant and positive economic impact, as per capita income increased 100% in Xidi and 398% in Hongcun between 1999 and 2007 (Jiang et al. 2009).

However, this economic prosperity has come at environmental, social, and cultural costs. Tourist arrivals to Xidi fluctuate greatly, both seasonally and daily. Most tourists visit between April and October, with arrivals peaking on Labor Day (May 1), National Day (October 1), and during the summer vacation period, from late July until early August. In addition, daily arrivals peak around noon, when it is not uncommon to have as many as 3, 000 visitors in the village, overwhelming local facilities (Lu et al. 2005: 583). This has created environmental problems such as increased wastewater discharge, solid waste disposal, and noise pollution (Li and Jin 2002; Liu 2008/2009). Wastewater from lodges and restaurants has polluted the

Fig. 6.5 Becoming a tourist attraction: the recently built Tibetan Quarter in Jiantang, Zhongdian County (renamed "Shangri La" in 2001), Yunnan province

ground water, and many of the 40 wells in the village have become unsafe for use (Lu et al. 2005).

Becoming a heritage attraction has negatively affected villager perceptions about their community. Tourists' conspicuous consumption, social problems such as public drunkenness, a wave of outside people opening tourist-related services, and a belief that public order has declined have all been reported by Chinese researchers. Tensions between local residents and outside business operators have led to frequent appeals by the latter to village and county officials, costing time and money and further exacerbating social animosities (Jiang et al. 2009: 28). In Xidi, villagers reported feeling that the tourist lifestyle did not fit their way of life, while in Hongcun and the neighboring village of Nanping, most families reported having members who left as migrant workers to seek opportunities elsewhere, an indication of low employment opportunities in the heritage tourism business (Li and Jin 2002: 19). A survey of local residents and visitors found that rapid commercialization had significantly affected the uniqueness and authenticity of the two ancient villages and the quality of life of the local villagers (Sun and Su 2004). Sun and Su (2004) reported that the presence of neon lights and rooftop solar panels did not fit with the sense of place for these heritage sites, while some local residents had decided to rent their homes to outside business people and move (Jin 2008). This once again demonstrates the "hollowing" phenomenon found in urban heritage destinations such as Lijiang, albeit on a smaller scale (Fig. 6.5).

Studies of other cultural heritage sites have shown a similar social and cultural impact on destination communities. Pingyao, a small city in northern Shanxi province that was able to maintain its Ming-era city walls and architecture by what in hindsight appears to have been an historical accident, was inscribed on the world heritage list in 1997. Relatively isolated and never of military or economic importance, Pingyao was sparred damage during the war against Japan and the civil war that followed as well as Maoist urban construction projects. However, in response to decentralization policies that placed the onus for funding on local bureaucracies, local officials targeted the town as a tourist resource. Their plans focused on restoring the city walls, decreasing the number of residents within the walls, and increasing and improving tourist facilities (Wang 2012: 4). Subsequently, the population within the walls was cut from 45,000 to 22,000 by 2008, mainly by forcing state services and enterprises to relocate outside the city walls. In addition, new zoning ordinances forced out local businesses that met the daily needs of residents and replaced these with tourist businesses. Finally, a ticket system for admission to local sites was introduced, effectively pricing out local residents (ibid, 12–13). Other research suggests that most local residents have not benefitted economically from these changes. In particular, residents living in the old town report a strong antagonism toward the local government due to relocation policies that have provided inadequate compensation for their homes and businesses. They have also been critical of what they see as an overcommercialization of the city and unethical business practices by outsiders (Wei and Zheng 2009). The net affect has been to transform the social fabric of Pingyao's center into a tourist and heritage space in which local residents are strangers.

This estrangement is evident at other sites as well. In a comparative study of the economic, social, cultural, and environmental impact of world heritage status on 12 Chinese communities situated at natural, cultural, and mixed-use sites, a majority of local residents who were surveyed agreed that tourism development had positive impacts on the local economy, improved heritage conservation, and raised peoples' awareness of heritage protection. But they also identified tourism as the main factor for driving up local prices, which in turn affected their quality of life. Tourism was also blamed for overcrowding and traffic congestion, noise and air pollution, and increased crime rates (Zou and Zheng 2012: 30–31). Residents also cited the harm on the environment caused by hotel and tourist facilities overbuilding. It is interesting to note that residents at cultural heritage sites had the lowest recognition of any positive economy impact on their community among the three types of world heritage sites and had strong negative perceptions of the social impact brought by tourism development (Zou and Zheng 2012: 32).

This leads to the most pressing question for heritage preservation, conservation, and construction projects: who owns heritage? If this is a collective good, to what extent do all members of society have a stake? To what extent do actually existing residents of a community have a right to participate in heritage conversations and decision making? Liberal political theory suggests that decentralizing political authority broadens the conversation about governance issues such as this. In other words, when decision making occurs at the local level, liberal political theory assumes this will reflect local interests, aspirations, and desires. Yet the political decentralization that has occurred in China in the last decade has not led to increased community participation, mainly because decision making remains vested in one political party. In addition, while the central government has ceded much authority to provincial and local authorities, it has also slashed direct funding to lower government levels. In regard to heritage management, this has had two effects. First, local authorities tend to view cultural and natural sites and objects not in terms of preservation or conservation but as development resources. Second, and as a direct consequence of the above, local state funding has been targeted at heritage sites and objects that are viewed as potentially profitable. This in turn has led to the outsourcing of heritage, as local authorities establish lucrative partnerships with private interests to develop, manage, and in some cases stage heritage (Wang 2012).

One potentially positive note is the increased presence of non-state organizations (NGOs) in the heritage debate. While NGOs are strictly controlled in China, two of the issues in which they have been allowed some scope are environmentalism and cultural heritage. Groups such as Friends of Nature, established in Beijing in 1994, and the Beijing Cultural Heritage Protection Center (CHP), established in 2003, have gained international attention, as well as funding, for their work. But nongovernment organizations in China function in a very different way than do their counterparts in liberal democracies. First, they tend to have close ties with specific parts of the state and regard the state as an ally against corporate interests (Yang 2009: 95). Thus, for example, the Beijing Cultural Heritage Protection Center became a legally registered NGO under the sponsorship of the Beijing Administration of Cultural Heritage, which from a liberal perspective is the state actor it should monitor (this would be equivalent to the federal Environmental Protection Agency in the United States sponsoring Greenpeace). Second, Chinese NGOs tend to focus on public education, not on conflict, and see themselves as advocates of increased public awareness of existing policies, not on contesting state policies (McClaren 2011). They also avoid politically loaded terms such as "campaign" (*yundong*) and "linking up" (*chuanlian*) – language that evokes political movements such as the Cultural Revolution – in favor of more technical terms such as "projects" (*xiangmu*) and "actions" (*xingdong*) (Yang 2009: 96–97). Overall, they emphasize working with authorities to ensure enforcement of existing regulations, not on working against the state.

Consequently, in situations in which local authorities increasingly partner with private capital to either use heritage sites as revenue sources or, as in the case of urban projects such as Beijing's Qianmen or Shanghai's Xintiandi, transform lived social space into historicized commercial zones, Chinese NGOs are ill-equipped to offer an effective response. CHP, for example, despite being China's most well-known cultural heritage NGO, has just three full-time employees (CHP 2012). And, even in situations in which it has been able to gain state support for historic preservation, this has not always stopped destruction. In 2009, CHP successfully lobbied the city's heritage administration to protect the former home of China's most famous twentieth-century architects, the couple Liang Sicheng and Lin Huiyin. Yet in early 2012, this small courtyard house was demolished to make way for a new commercial development (Jacobs 2012). This example illustrates not just the lack of influence even well-known NGOs have but also the conflicts between different parts of the state at various levels of governance. As long as local officials are required to generate their own revenue sources and demonstrate consistent economic growth, they will use their effective monopolies over land use in their jurisdictions to support real estate projects that displace residents, demolish existing built space, and consequently threaten the country's architectural heritage.

Bibliography

Aird, Sarah C. 2001. China's Three Gorges: The impact of dam construction on emerging human rights. *Human Rights Brief* 8(2): 24–26. 36–37.

Beattie, James. 2002. Dam building, dissent, and development: The emergence of the Three Gorges Project. *New Zealand Journal of Asian Studies* 4: 138–158.

Beijing Cultural Heritage Protection Center (CHP). 2012. About CHP. http://en.bjchp.org/?page_id=1392. Accessed 18 Aug 2012.

Bray, David. 2005. *Social space and governance in urban China*. Palo Alto: Stanford University Press.

Changxue, Liu. 2008/2009. A study on rural residents' perception of tourism impact and attitude towards tourism development. *Commercial Research* 377: 164–168.

Chen Yawei. 2007. Regeneration and sustainable development in China's transformation. ENHR International Conference on Sustainable Urban Areas, Rotterdam, 25–28 June 2007. http://www.enhr2007rotterdam.nl/documents/W19_paper_Chen.pdf. Accessed 17 Aug 2012

China National Tourism Administration (CNTA). 2008. Major statistics of Chinese tourism, Jan–Dec 2008. http://www.cnta.gov.cn/html/2009-2/2009-2-18-9-34-95871.html. Accessed 10 Oct 2011

China National Tourism Administration (CNTA). 2009. Foreign visitor arrivals by purpose, Jan–Dec 2009. http://cnto.org/chinastats_2009ArrivalsByPurpose.asp. Accessed 12 Oct 2011

Ching Kwan, Lee. 2007. *Against the law: Labor protests in China's Sunbelt and Rustbelt*. Berkeley: University of California Press.

Cuihua, Peng. 2010. Protection of traditional culture in the resettlement in the Three Gorges reservoir area. *Nationalities Forum* 9: 35–36.

Fan, Li, and Jin Zhongmin. 2002. A comparative analysis of tourism's impact on ancient villages in Southern Anhui Province: Xidi, Hongcun and Nanping. *Human Geography* 17(2): 17–21.

Global Heritage Fund. 2011. European Parliament calls on China to Halt destruction of ancient Kashgar. *Heritage on the Wire*, March 14. http://globalheritagefund.org/onthewire/blog/destruction_of_ancient_kashgar. Accessed 20 Aug 2012

Government of China (GOC). 2008a. State administration of cultural heritage. *Nomination Report for Mount Wutai* (Yang Rui, Editor in Chief), Beijing.

Government of China (GOC). 2008b. *Conversation and management plan for the nominated world heritage site of Mount Wutai*, Beijing.

Gruber, Stefan. 2007. Protecting China's cultural heritage sites in times of rapid change: Current developments, practice and law. *Asia Pacific Journal of Environmental Law* 253(10): 253–301.

Guobin, Yang. 2009. *The power of the Internet in China*. New York: Columbia University Press.

Guoping, Li, and Ye Wen. 2001. Influence of the Three Gorges Project on evolution of the Yangtze Three Gorges tourism layout and countermeasures. *Geography and Territorial Research* 17(4): 35–38. 43.

Haiping, Jiang, Wang Yanhua, and Li Jingbing. 2009. Research on development models of ancient villages based on community management: A case study of world cultural heritage in Xidi Village and Hongcun Village. *East China Economic Management* 23(8): 24–28.

Hammer, Joshua. 2010. Demolishing Kashgar's history. *Smithsonian* March. http://www. smithsonianmag.com/history-archaeology/Demolishing-Kashgars-History. html#ixzz246Gg0zSc. Accessed 20 Aug 2012.

International Council on Monuments and Sites (ICOMOS). 2011. *Heritage at risk: ICOMOS world report 2008–2010 on monuments and sites in danger*. Berlin: Hendrick Bahler.

Jacobs, Andrew. 2012. In Beijing's building Frenzy, even an 'Immovable Cultural Relic' is not safe. *The New York Times*, February 3. http://www.nytimes.com/2012/02/05/world/asia/in-beijing-razing-of-historic-house-stirs-outrage.html?pagewanted=all. Accessed 18 Aug 2012.

Jin Zhongmin. 2008. Analysis of economic and social impact of tourism on community-based world heritage sites: The case of ancient villages of Xidi and Hongcun in Southern Anhui Province. *Digital China*. http://www.china001.com/show_hdr.php?xname=PPDDMV0&dname =OIHN341&xpos=110. Accessed 18 July 2012.

Jing, Sun, and Su Qin. 2004. Visual influence and management for ancient villages. *Human Geography* 19(r4): 38–40.

Jue, Huang, Zhang Tianxin, and Takayoshi Yamamura. 2009. A study of the tourism commerce population and spatial distribution in the old town of Lijiang. *Chinese Landscape Architecture* 5: 23–26.

Kunfu, Jiang, Zhang Shulin, Cheng Peng, and Tang Weiliang. 2009. Research on the cultural geography of the Three Gorges. *Journal of Jingchu University of Technology* 24(5): 92–96.

Layton, Kelly. 2007. Qianmen, gateway to a Beijing heritage. *China Heritage Quarterly* 12 (December). http://chinaheritagenewsletter.anu.edu.au/articles.php?searchterm=012_qianmen. inc&issue=012. Accessed 17 Aug 2012.

Le Mentec, Katlana. 2006. The Three Gorges Dam project – Religious practices and heritage conservation: A study of cultural remains and local popular religion in the Xian of Yunyang (Municipality of Chongqing). *China Perspectives* 65: 2–14.

Lu Xiaobo, and Elizabeth Perry. 1997. Introduction. In *Danwei: The Changing Chinese Workplace in Historical and Comparative Perspective*, ed. Lu and Perry. Armonk,: M.E. Sharpe.

McLaren, Anne. 2011. Environment and cultural heritage in China: Introduction. *Asian Studies Review* 35: 429–437.

Murphy, J.D. 1994. An annotated chronological index of People's Republic of China statutory and other materials relating to cultural property. *International Journal of Cultural Property* 3: 159–168.

Ning, Yuan, Huang Na, Zhang Long, Fan Wenjing, and Sun Keqin. 2012. Evaluation of tourism resources based on AHP method in ancient villages – A case of world heritage sites of Xidi and Hongcun. *Resource Development & Market* 28(2): 179–181.

Nyíri, Pal. 2009. Between encouragement and control: Tourism, modernity and discipline in China. In *Asia on tour: Exploring the rise of Asian tourism*, ed. Tim Winter, Peggy Teo, and T.C. Chang, 153–169. London: Routledge.

Ponseti, Marta and Jordi López-Pujol. 2006. The Three Gorges Dam project in China: History and consequences. *Revista HMIC* (IV), pp. 151–188

Qifu, Wu, and Wang Ruhui. 2007. Review of research on the old town of Lijiang. *Tourism Science* 21(1): 17–21.

Qingrong, Shu, and Chen Hua. 2010. A discussion on protecting historical relics in the Three Gorges reservoir area. *Yangtze River* 41(23): 83–86.

Shepherd, Robert. 2012. *Faith in heritage: Displacement, development, and religious tourism in contemporary China*. Walnut Grove: Left Coast Press.

Shuyi, Wang. 2012. From a living city to a world heritage site: Authorized heritage conservation and development and its impact on the local community. *International Development Planning Review* 34(1): 1–17.

Song, Lu, Lu Lin, Xu Ming, Liang Dongdong, Wang Li, Wang Yong, and Yang Zhao. 2005. Tourism environmental carrying capacity of ancient villages: A case study of the world cultural heritage site of Xidi Village. *Geographical Research* 24(4): 581–590.

Svensson, Marina. 2006. *In the ancestor's shadow: Cultural heritage contestations in Chinese villages*. Working Paper #16. Stockholm: Centre for East and Southeast Asian Studies, Lund University.

Tanfeng, Tang. 1998. Treasures of the Three Gorges: Lack of funds to rescue. *Voice of Chinese Worldwide* 7: 9–10.

Thapa, Brijesh. 2010. Funding strategies for world heritage sites in least developed countries. In *Cultural heritage management: A global perspective*, ed. Phyllis Messenger and George Smith, 278–294. Gainsville: University of Florida.

Tongqian, Zou, and Zheng Chunhui. 2012. Perception difference of tourism impact among residents at different heritage sites. *Tourism Forum* 5(1): 29–33.

Wei, Hong, and Zheng Yaoxing. 2009. The impact of tourism development on local residents – A case study of Pingyao ancient city. *Economic Research* 25: 147–148.

Weller, Robert. 2006. *Discovering nature: Globalization and environmental culture in China and Taiwan*. Cambridge: Cambridge University Press.

Womack, Brantly. 1991. Transfigured community: Neo-traditionalism and work-unit socialism in China. *China Quarterly* 126: 313–332.

Xiuqing, Li. 1999. Coordinative development of the preservation of cultural relics and tourism. *Resources and Environment in the Yangtze Basin* 8(1): 30–37.

Yan, Liu. 2005. Social and cultural impacts of tourism development on Lijiang ancient city. *Yunnan Geographical Environment Research* 17: 29–32.

Yanna, Li, and Zhang Hui. 2006. Ideas for tourism marketing of ancient villages in Southern Anhui Province: The case of world heritage sites of Xidi and Hongcun. *Journal of Higher Correspondence Education* 20(2): 41–44.

Yardley, Jim. 2006. Olympics imperil historic Beijing neighborhood. *New York Times*, July 12. http://www.nytimes.com/2006/07/12/world/asia/12beijing.html?_r=1&pagewanted=all. Accessed 17 Aug 2012

Zhuang, Kongshao. 1999. Protection and practice of ethnic folk cultural heritage in the Yangtze Three Gorges area. *Journal of Central Minority Nationality University* 5: 128–138.

Conclusion

We close with a practical dilemma, the historical reality of China. A relatively small area of present-day China has been continuously and intensively inhabited for thousands of years. Population density, lack of open land, and improved technologies mean that new construction takes place on top of the material past. In short, much of the built space of China's historical heartland is a heritage site. This raises a practical question: what should be excavated and preserved in such a situation? How to balance the material development needs of the present with historical preservation in a country in which material artifacts are potentially so common?

As we have explained in this book, the heritage process in China demonstrates both the limits of central government authority and the realities of a complex field of power within the PRC, driven by continual rapid economic development. A growing domestic tourism industry, significant environmental damage, and large-scale construction projects pose further challenges to preserving China's material and natural cultural heritage (Grubber 2007). Moreover, a growing threat to heritage is the illegal excavation and selling of cultural relics, a problem exacerbated by the increasingly decentralized political structure. In 1987, within a few years of the start of the economic reform movement, the State Council issued a decree banning the unauthorized excavation and sale of artifacts. A year later, the Sixth People's Congress approved the death penalty for serious smuggling of cultural artifacts, and in 1991 the State Council issued a second decree that sought to stop unauthorized tomb excavations (Murphy 1994).

In a paradoxical way, these current problems mirror the key threats to heritage preservation in China before 1949, when foreigners routinely excavated and removed a wide range of material artifacts that remain abroad in both public and private collections. However, the market for artifacts is now driven by domestic demand, as a small but exceedingly wealthy elite turns its gaze towards the arts and culture. These problems have been exacerbated by the current state campaign to "Go West" aimed at developing interior provinces, as infrastructural and other projects in these less economically developed areas often uncover archeological sites and artifacts. Local officials have few incentives to protect such sites because to do so usually requires

R.J. Shepherd and L. Yu, *Heritage Management, Tourism, and Governance in China:*
Managing the Past to Serve the Present, SpringerBriefs in Archaeology 2,
DOI 10.1007/978-1-4614-5918-7, © Springer Science+Business Media, LLC 2013

significant funding from the local and provincial levels as well as sometimes curtailing specific development projects. This situation is exacerbated by the fact that personal promotion for local officials is largely based on their success at demonstrating economic growth. Hence, many officials promote short-term economic development results, which is hardly conducive to heritage preservation. At best, this leads to a focus on using heritage sites as tourist attractions, which often poses new challenges, as success in attracting heavy tourist volume may place fragile sites at risk.

Finally, the lack of influence in heritage decision making by local communities, preservationists, archeologists, architects, and historians means that economic motives will continue to trump all else. If the Qianmen model persists, more and more historic neighborhoods will be razed and replaced by pseudo-historical commercial spaces, leading to the distinct possibility that "socialism with Chinese characteristics," the party's euphemism for the current hypermodernization campaign, will lead to even greater destruction of China's cultural heritage than occurred during the worst of the Cultural Revolution. Red Guards used pickaxes and hammers to attack religious and other sites; real estate developers use bulldozers.

There is, in summary, no easy answer to the dilemma faced by every society that seeks to balance preserving the past with improving the material realities of its contemporary citizens. Indeed, China serves as an extreme example of this dilemma, as PRC authorities must grapple with the largest population in the world on a landmass that has been continuously inhabited for thousands of years by a highly developed civilization.

Bibliography

Grubber, Stefan. 2007. Protecting China's cultural heritage sites in times of rapid change: Current developments, practice and law. *Asia Pacific Journal of Environmental Law* 253(10): 253–301.
Murphy, J.D. 1994. An annotated chronological index of People's Republic of China statutory and other materials relating to cultural property. *International Journal of Cultural Property* 3: 159–168.

Index

A
Admissions economy, 57
Alexandria, Virginia's Old Town, 73
Anthropocosmic, 35
Archeological sites, 75
Archeology, 9, 14

B
Badaling, 59
Beihai Park, 5
Beijing Administration of Cultural
  Heritage, 80
Bifengxia, 51
Bogutu, 6
Buddhism, 36
Bureau of religious affairs, 52

C
CCP. *See* Chinese Communist Party (CCP)
Central Commission for Building Spiritual
  Civilization, 37
Central Park, 70
Chengde, 28, 40, 62, 63, 64
Chiang Kaishek, 10, 15
China Central Spiritual Civilization
  Steering Committee, 29
China National Tourism Administration
  (CNTA), 49, 61
China National Tourism Organization
  (CNTO), 48
Chinatown, 73
Chinese Communist Party (CCP), 1
Civil society, 38

CNTA. *See* China National Tourism
  Administration (CNTA)
Commercialization, 78
Communist Party, 13, 14, 16, 19, 27
Confucian, 7, 38
Confucianism, 34
Confucius, 6
Creek Park, 70
Cultural heritage, 52
Cultural heritage management, 50
Cultural heritage protection (CHP), 80
Cultural preservation, 36
Cultural relics, 48
Cultural Relics Bureau, 15
Cultural revolution, 16, 30, 35, 36
  had many positive effects, 17
  was to education, 19
Culture, 39

D
Dalai Lama, 15, 20
Datong, 74
Deng Xiaoping, 37
Displacement, 70
Dr. Sun Yat-sen, 6

E
Eastern Han, 21
Emperor Qianlong, 62
Environmental, 34
Environmentalism, 34, 80
Environmental Protection Agency, 80
Ethnic tourism, 2

R.J. Shepherd and L. Yu, *Heritage Management, Tourism, and Governance in China:*
Managing the Past to Serve the Present, SpringerBriefs in Archaeology 2,
DOI 10.1007/978-1-4614-5918-7, © Springer Science+Business Media, LLC 2013

F
Faneuil Hall, 73
Five relationships, 8
    and three bonds of
        Confucianism, 27
Forbidden City, 5, 10, 19, 57, 59
Four olds, 16, 17
Fredrick Engels, 13
Friends of nature, 80

G
Gang of Four, 18
Gao Yuan, 17
Gaslight district in San Diego, 73
Genghis Khan, 5
Geological survey of China, 8
Globalization, 33, 47
Great Hall of the People, 15
Great leap forward, 16, 36
Great Wall, 19, 57
Greenpeace, 80
Gu Jiegang, 18
Gulangyu, 15

H
Han, 8, 25, 26, 39
Han dynasty, 28
Henry Lewis Morgan, 13
Heritage, 1, 2, 13, 20, 39, 47
Heritage preservation, 50
Historical materialist, 39
Historiography, 13
Hohhot, 74
Hollowing, 77
Hongcun, 77, 78
Hoover Dam, 36
Huangshan, 51, 61
Huashan, 70
Huizong, 40
Hu Jintao, 37
Humaneness *(ren)*, 38
Hu Shi, 18

I
ICOMOS, 74
Iconoclasm of the cultural revolution, 18
Impact the cultural revolution had on cultural
        heritage, 16
Inner Mongolian Museum, 21
Intangible, 2
Intangible heritage practice, 2

J
Jade Buddha Temple, 59
Jingangku, 70
Jingshan, 7
Jingshen, 6
Jinhua, 42
Jiuzhaigou, 56
Jiuzhaigou National Park, 54, 57, 59
Johan Andersson, 14
Johan Gunnar Andersson, 9
John Dewey, 18
Jung Chang, 17
Jurchen, 5

K
Kaifeng, 5
Kanding, 28
Kangxi, 40
Kang Xi Emperor, 62
Kaogutu, 6
Kashgar, 74
KMT, 9, 10
Kublai Khan, 28
Kunming, 74

L
Lake Bita, 43
Leshan, 55, 56
Lhasa, 15, 28
Liang Sicheng, 80
Li Chi, 9
Lijiang, 28, 57, 58, 76, 77
Lijiang Model, 76
Lin Huiyin, 80
Lu Dalin, 6
Lungshan, 14

M
Management transfer model, 51
Mao, 36
Mao Zedong, 10
Marx, 36
Material culture, 40
Mausoleum of Qin Shi Huangdi, 19
Ming Dynasty, 5
Ministry of Civil Affairs, 53
Ministry of Construction, 48, 52
Ministry of Culture, 52
Ministry of Geology, 53
Ministry of Housing and Urban–Rural
        Development, 52

Ministry of Land and Resources, 53
Minzu, 8, 37
Modernization is viewed by CCP, 29
Mogao Caves, 57
Morality, 19
Mount Emei, 7, 51, 56
Mount Tai (Taishan), 19, 57, 70
Mount Taibai, 43
Mount Wutai, 7, 28, 53, 54, 59, 70
Mount Wutai National Park, 42
Museum display, 2

N
Nanjing, 5
National Historical and Cultural Cities, 48
National Museum of China, 21, 37, 59
National Museum of History, 3
National Park Model, 51
National scenic areas, 48
National Tourism Administration, 53
National tourism policies, 2
Naxi, 76
New culture movement, 3, 18
NGOs, 80
Nien Cheng, 17
1911 Revolution, 6, 7
1972 Convention on world heritage, 53
Norbulingka, 15
Northern song, 76

P
Paleoanthropology, 25
Party (KMT), 8
Peasants, 68
Peking Man, 19, 26
Pilgrimage, 48
Pingyao, 57, 58, 79
Potala Palace, 20, 28
Preservation, 47

Q
Qianlong, 40
Qianmen, 25, 72, 73, 80
Qianmen model, 73
Qin Dynasty Terracotta Warrior Museum, 59
Qing, 21
Qing Dynasty, 7, 72
Qing Shihuang, 57
Qing Summer Resort, 62
Qizilchoqa, 26

R
Ren, 8
Republic of China, 8

S
SACH. *See* State administration
    for cultural Heritage (SACH);
    State administration of cultural
    heritage (SACH)
Scenic spots, 6, 43
Shang, 14
Shang Dynasty, 7
Shanghai, 59
Shao Lin, 50
Shikumen houses, 73
Shui On Property Group, 73
Sino-Japanese War, 20
SOHO Corporation, 72
Song, 5
Song Dynasty, 6
Song Shan Scenic Area, 51
Songze Monastery, 41
Soviet Union, 36
Spiritual civilization campaign, 37
Spiritual development, 39
Spiritual' *(jingshen)* development, 40
Spring and Autumn period, 21
Stakeholder, 71
State Administration of Cultural Heritage
    (SACH), 2, 17, 20, 25, 27, 49,
    50, 52, 75
State Council, 15, 17, 48
State Forestry Administration, 53
Sui, 21
Sun Yat-sen, 7, 8, 18, 25, 39, 74
Suzhi, 38, 40
Suzhi and wenming, 40

T
Taihuai, 70, 71
Tang, 7
Tang Dynasty, 21, 55
Tangible heritage, 2
Temple of Heaven, 59
Tennessee Valley Authority, 36
Terracotta Army, 57
Three Gorges Dam, 74
Three Principles of the People, 8
Tiananmen square, 15, 30, 59
Ti-yong, 36
Tong Meng Hui, 8

Tourism, 47, 48
Tourism development, 79

U
Uighurs, 21, 74
UNESCO, 35, 51, 57, 69, 74
UNESCO World Heritage Commission, 52
United Nation, 2
United States land institute, 73

W
Wang Binghua, 26
Wang Fu, 6
Wenhua (culture), 38
Wenming, 29, 35, 37
Western Hills, 59
West Lake, 59, 70
Wong Tai Sin, 42
Work units, 67, 68
World heritage list, 57, 58
World heritage movements, 34
World heritage sites, 2
World union of conservation, 69
Wulingyuan, 52
Wuzong emperor, 17

X
Xanadu, 28
Xiahe, 28
Xiamen, 15
Xidi, 77
Xinjiang mummies, 26
Xintiandi, 25, 73, 80

Y
Yangshao, 9, 14
Yellow Mountain, 60, 70
Yellowstone, 70
Yuan dynasty, 5

Z
Zhang Fei temple, 76
Zhangjiajie National Park, 52
Zhaojun, 28
Zhongdian, 28, 41
Zhou, 5, 14
Zhou Enlai, 17
Zhoukoudian, 26, 59
Zhoukoudian Peking
        Man, 50, 57
Zi ran, 34

Printed by Printforce, the Netherlands